W9-CSO-939

BICYCLES
Austin's Racing & Mountain Bike Specialists Since 1971

SPECIALIZED. TREK
LEMOND
KLEIN FUJI

Huge Selection of Parts and Accessories
Helmets, Clothing, Shoes and Bags
Yakima and Thule Car Racks

473-8700

Hours:	Th. 12-8
Mon. 10-6	Fri. 10-6
Tues. 10-6	Sat. 10-5
Wed. Closed	Sun. Closed

2401 San Gabriel

WATERLOO CYCLES

WELCOME TO
KONA WORLD

Texas' First
Authorized Kona
Dealer

Not What You Think

We're around **the corner**
from our old **location.** We're
now at 2815 **Fruth,** ½ block
east of Guadalupe & 29th.
We've got **easier access,** a
better layout, **even better**
service and **lower rent.**
That's allowed **us to drop**
our prices **on bikes about**
15% and **parts and**
accessaries **as much as**
35%--*All Day, Every Day.*

29th

Fruth

NEW Location
2815 Fruth

Store Hours:
Mon.-Sat.10-6:00
Thurs.   10-8:00
Sun.   noon-5:00
Call: 47-CYCLE

Guadalupe

Old
Location

Acknowledgements

Special thanks to Tricky-D, Flowerchild, Scooter, Pepitto, Pablo, and Pressuremon for scouting out the original trails with us.

The MAD House advertising agency, especially Larry McIntosh, was instrumental in the creation of this way-cool-souped-up of version of the book. Muchas gracias.

The awesome cover design is by Robert Lin, who did an excellent job while working with two people who kept remembering things that needed to be included at the last minute.

Some of the killer photos were taken by Monkey Boy aka Steve Chandler and we appreciate his climbing, running, and creative skills.

Printing History

First Edition	1993
Second Edition	1994
Third Edition	1996
Fourth Edition	1999
Fifth Edition	2002

Copyright © 1993, 1994, 1996, 1999, 2002 - All rights reserved.
No portion of *Mountain Biking Central Texas* may be reproduced without the expressed, written consent of the authors.

ISBN 0-9671018-1-6

Ragged Edge Riders
P.O. Box 161862
Austin, TX 78767

The authors and publisher have made every effort to ensure the accuracy of information contained in this book, but can accept no liability for any loss, injury or inconvenience sustained by anybody as a result of information or advice contained in this guide.

Mountain Biking Central Texas

Becky Youman
Rick Youman

Ragged Edge Riders

4

UNIVERSITY CYCLERY

EST. **1977**

AUSTIN, TEXAS

Bike Sales/Repairs   Bike Rentals
2901 N. Lamar   474-6696

OZONE Bike Dept

Yeti   Marin   LOOK   Masi
Redline   HARO   Free Agent   KHS

3202-C Guadalupe· Austin·TX ·78705· (512)302-1164
www.ozonebikes.com

TABLE OF CONTENTS

Introduction

Austin Rides

6

WE'VE GOT THE GEAR...

YOU PICK THE TRAIL.

CANNONDALE • DIAMONDBACK • GARY FISHER • GIANT • RALEIGH

Free Lifetime Service Contract on All Bike Purchases • Not All Brands Available at All Locations

Sun & Ski Sports
The Gear. The Advice. The Price.

AUSTIN: 2438 W. Anderson Ln. (Across from Northcross Mall) 512-467-2782 DALLAS: Grapevine Mills Hwy 121 (Just north of D/FW Airport) 972-355-9424 • 5500 Greenville Ave. Old Town Ctr (Corner of Greenville and Lover's Lane) 214-696-2696 SAN ANTONIO: 13411 San Pedro Avenue (281 & Bitters Rd., next to Party City) 210-494-0429 HOUSTON: Katy Mills (I-10 & 90) 281-644-6040 • 6100 Westheimer (Between Hillcroft & Chimney Rock) 713-783-8180 • Memorial City Mall (I-10 at Gessner Rd.) 713-464-6363 • 5503 FM 1960 W (At Champion Forest Dr.) 281-537-0928 • 1355 Bay Area Blvd. (In the Target Shopping Center) 281-316-1365 www.sunandski.com

wherever you go.....GO PREPARED!!
.....WITH OUR SUPERB COLLECTION OF BIKE BAGS, PACKS & ACCESSORIES; CAMPING & TRAVEL TOOLS, CLOTHING, FOOTWEAR AND MORE.

Whole Earth Provision Co.
2410 San Antonio - 478-1577 • 1014 N. Lamar Blvd. 476- 1414 • Westgate/CM Hwy 290 @ S Lamar 899-0992

CONTENTS (continued)

Day Trippin'

8

Austin's Newest & Largest

CYCLE 360

Extended Test Ride Program

The Best Values, Service & Selection

THE BEST DEAL ON TWO WHEELS

Do a 180 to Cycle 360!

With Cycle 360's <u>low price guarantee</u>, there's no need to forego the best service and selection in central Texas to get the <u>best</u> <u>prices</u> on new bikes and accessories. Don't be fooled by our high-dollar location, we have <u>fantastic</u> <u>prices</u> on a fantastic selection of fantastic merchandise!

Cycle 360 was voted *"Best Young, Upwardly Mobile Bicycle Shop"* in the latest *Best of Austin* readers' poll. Apparently Austin Chronicle readers appreciate and recognize a <u>great</u> <u>deal</u> when they see one!

Discover for yourself the best kept secret in cycling. Fantastic service, selection and <u>low</u> <u>prices</u> can come together under one roof ... in a fantastic location! Visit us today in the beautiful Davenport Village Shopping Center; the best bike store location in Austin!

Home of Outrageous Customer Service

Road * Mountain * Triathlon Specialists

Unconditional Money Back Satisfaction Guarantee

Mon – Fri 9a - 7p
Sat 10a- 6p
Sun. 12 - 6

306-8778
www.cycle360.com

3801 N. Capital of TX Hwy
at Westlake Drive
in Davenport Village

CONTENTS (continued)

Locator Maps

Extras

INTRODUCTION

Mountain biking is fun. That's really all there is behind the upsurge in mountain bike sales and the expansion of fat tire floor space in bike stores around the world. Sure, it's a good way to stay fit, it's relatively inexpensive once you get the basic equipment and even most couch potatoes know how to ride bikes, but the thing that keeps us coming back is pure, high octane, *estupendo* fun.

This book is designed to be a guide for mountain bikers of all levels and experience. The point is to get you out on the trails in Central Texas. It's nice to ride on the street every once in a while (so you remember why you love trail riding so much), but cars, exhaust and Bubbas get old quickly. That's why we're here.

Mountain biking lets you get outside and enjoy the fine scenery and weather of Central Texas. Only a Joneser wouldn't jump at the chance to get a great workout in the best gym around – Mother Nature's.

For those of you whose off-road experience consists of hopping the curb, you are going to freak over the feeling of whooshing down a single track trail through the trees (Remember that scene from *Return of the Jedi* where they're zooming through the redwoods on flying motorcycles? That's what it's like.)

Even you old pros will probably find a new trail or two in here. Expand your adventures and check out one of our day trip destinations that you've never ridden before.

Everybody will dig the food, drink, and swimming hole recommendations. Sometimes that's our favorite part of the ride. So, put on your helmet, grab your bike and follow us *compadres*.

HOW TO USE THIS BOOK

This handy dandy little guide is so easy to use that even if you've tested the limits of your helmets you should be able to figure it out. We have a section on rides in the Austin area and another on day trip destinations. The majority of the day trip rides are within a couple of hours of Austin.

Each ride description is a page long to keep things simple and there is always a map on the facing page in case you can't read. Actually, if you can't read you should have someone else read it to you, because there is some pretty useful stuff in each write up.

Contact Information

Some of the trails, especially those in the day trip section, are closed one or two days a week. We have listed that info in here, but it's always a good idea to call ahead to make sure schedules haven't changed. It would suck to get all psyched about a ride, get out there, and find a lock on the gate.

If the destination has a website, we have included that also. Some websites over up-to-date information on the status of the trail

Remember that unimproved trails are closed for at least 24 hours after a rain.

The Rating System

This book is divided into sections of easy, moderate and difficult rides. For comparison sake, my brother and I rated all the rides. He's a hammerhead rider and I'm not so everyone is covered.

Easy: You'd better be able to do these rides or your mother wears combat boots and all those other second grade taunts. These rides aren't that much harder than riding on pavement as they have well-packed dirt and are neither too long nor too hilly.

Intermediate: These rides are sure to put a smile on your face. They will give you a good work out, a few cheap thrills and a sense of accomplishment, but they won't kick your @$$.

Difficult: Grunt, wail, and feel adrenaline rushes not unlike the Mountain Dew commercials. These rides are guaranteed to pump you up, but they can also bring you down to earth quickly (i.e. face plant) and wear you out.

The Low Down

The body of each write-up has the dope on each ride. Some have mileage sections to give you a sense of where you are and how far you have come. If you have a computer and your mileage doesn't exactly jive with ours...oh well. All computers were not created equal.

Most of these trails are pretty well marked or well used so hopefully you won't get lost. If you do, you can always turn around and go back the way you came. Some of the rides have very well marked trails so for those we don't go into detail on finding specific twists and turns.

Water, Food and Refreshment

Biking in Texas in the warmer months can make you one hot *tamale*. There's nothing better than a quick dip in some cool pool to revive you after a ride so we've included directions to the nearest swimming hole with each ride description.

After bringing your core temperature down you should satisfy some other primal urges (not that one potty-brain). We have included eateries with good fare and, as important, killer character for your drinking and dining delight. We've also even thrown in a handful of taverns and pool halls for your continued entertainment.

How To Get There

We thought it would be a good idea to tell you how to get to the trailhead of these rides so we've included that on each page. Our starting place is always Austin High School near 1st (Caesar Chaves) and Lamar. Keep that in mind when we tell you how to get somewhere. There are rough maps of Austin and Central Texas in the back of the book that are marked with all the rides to give you an idea of the general vicinity of each one.

Maps

Okay, here's where some disclaimers come in. These maps are sketches of the trails to get you pointed in the right direction and complement the text, but they are not divinely inspired. Trails change over time, landmarks fall and now you can't sue us if you get lost. You're big boys and girls so use your finely tuned sense of direction and pay attention as you ride. If worst comes to worst you can leave the way you came.

LISTEN TO YOUR MOTHER

Speaking of using your noggin'... mountain biking can be risky and there are some things you need to do to minimize scar tissue. These are not suggestions, these are rules to help keep you safe. Mountain bikers have a bad reputation for harming trails and themselves. We'll get to minimizing trail damage later – this section will help you minimize damage to your own bag of bones.

- Thou shalt **WEAR A HELMET**.
There is no excuse for ignoring this one. Wear it, love it, live it or you might die.

- Thou **DON'T RIDE ALONE** on little used trails.
A broken collarbone ten miles from your car with no one around can be a bummer. It also makes you look very irresponsible.

- Thou shalt **BRING LOTS OF WATER**.
It gets hot in these parts pardner and dehydration is not an attractive alternative. Fill up the Camelbak and more. You should take at least two quarts per person on every trip.

- Thou shalt **CARRY A TOOL KIT**.
We've got a whole section on this one...read on.

- Thou shalt **STAY IN CONTROL**.
If you are in control you are in less danger of hurting yourself, and more importantly, of hurting or scaring others.

In addition to these five commandments (so we're no Moses), there are some other things that it would behoove you to keep in mind for your safety: wear sunscreen, carry a small first aid kit, carry some food, pay attention to the weather and love your neighbor.

TOOLS OF THE TRADE

Imagine hammering up the surreal petrified sand dunes of Moab, Utah and having your seat become so loose that you cannot ride without the point of it giving you an enema. It happened to a friend of mine who left his allen wrench sitting on the car...it's ugly, don't let it happen to you.

If you have the right tools and know how to use them you can prevent a lot of heart (and butt) ache. A good bike tool kit will include the following:

- pump and extra tubes
- patch kit and tire irons
- Swiss army knife
- allen wrenches
- chain tool and spare chain link
- extra spokes and spoke wrench
- screw driver
- pliers
- crescent wrench
- lubricant (not KY you goose)

Those James Bond "twenty tools in one" sold in bike stores are a compact way to carry many of these tools. Some optional implements that you might or might not want along include toilet paper and a corkscrew or bottle opener.

We hate fixing flats, so in thorny areas we use Slime Lite tubes...barely any extra weight and great protection against punctures.

The most tricked out tools in the world won't do squat for you if you don't know how to use them. Spend some time at home reading your bike manual or maybe even carry a small repair guide with you.

Fashion Plates

Some other "tools" that can make biking a lot more enjoyable are biker specific gear. While you don't need to Lycrafy your body to enjoy biking, there's a reason a lot of these things were invented.

We've rated the following items in our own order of importance so you can figure out how deep to dive.

· Bike and Helmet

Mandatory.

· Protective Eyewear

This is also important. You can wear your cheap sunglasses or your swim goggles, but make sure your eyes are protected from limbs and bugs. You can spring for the Oakleys later.

· Gloves

Definitely worth the $10. They make your hands more comfortable when you ride and protect you when you come off the bike.

· Bike Shorts

These also add a lot in the comfort area. After a few hours in the saddle your hiney will be thanking you. You don't have to "leave nothing to the imagination" anymore. There are lots of great baggy shorts with a padded inner layer.

Yo Jill, don't settle for Jack's leftovers. You'll find mountain biking clothes cut specifically for women at the bike shops that carry larger inventories.

· Bike Shoes

These aren't necessary until you become more advanced, but when you get them you'll never go back. Until then, wear the stiffest soled shoes you have.

BIKING 101

You learned to ride your bike when you were six and zipped all around the neighborhood. In junior high your bike was your main set of wheels. You rode it some in high school, but only when you couldn't get your hands on a car. Since then biking has been a way to get some exercise or enjoy a sunny day. Now you want to try this mountain biking thang. No problemo. If you can ride a bike, you can mountain bike.

T'aint Quite The Same

There are, however, some things about mountain biking that make it different from zooming around the cul-de-sac. The main thing is pavement, or lack there of.

Pavement is smooth, big, wide and offers great traction. The best mountain biking trails are skinny, dirt covered and full of obstacles. That's what makes it so much fun. You're thinking about balance and getting by, over and around objects instead of how much your legs and lungs hurt.

The only way to improve your biking skills is to spend time in the saddle. (Well, make that spending time in and out of the saddle.) You'll definitely biff a time or two as you ride increasingly difficult trails. We consider scars badges of honor, but don't recommend breaking bones.

You can use some of the advice below to bunny-hop your way up the learning curve.

Staying on the Trail

The key to mountain biking is sticking to your line. (In other words...making the bike go the direction you want it to.) It's harder than you think. When you first start out you may find yourself swerving around like a drunken sailor. Don't worry. That's normal.

Try these hints to maintain control of your bike:

• Do not focus on obstacles you want to avoid but rather direct your eyes to the line you want to travel. Your bike will amazingly follow suit. It sounds simplistic, but it works.

• Keep your gaze a good twenty to thirty feet beyond your front tire instead of right on top of those knobbies. It will help you anticipate what's coming up next.

• Keep your hands on the grips and feet on the pedals. Duh. Bumps in the trails will knock your feet off the pedals unless you have your dogs attached with toe clips. Just make sure you have practiced getting in and out of them so that you can do it in a hurry.

Getting Up Hills

When humping up those hills on the street you are used to standing up on the bike. Try that mountain biking and you generally find yourself spinning your wheels. When mountain biking, your tires needs to be weighted in order get gription on the loamy trail.

• Stay seated when climbing hills with your weight over your back tire. If you find your front wheel coming off the ground or losing its grip, use your upper body to weight it as well. Stay low so that your chest is practically parallel to your top tube. (Exception: On long hills with small inclines you can stand from time to time.)

• As you make your way up a hill, change gears BEFORE it gets too hard to pedal. This way you keep your mo' going.

• Try to keep your upper body steady with minimal side to side movement. This is not the time to do the funky chicken.

Getting Down Hills

Gravity is your friend, but you have to learn to work with it. The force of nature seems to like nothing better than to pull you over the front of your bike and send you tumbling down the trail. That's no fun.

• Lower your seat when going down steep hills and keep your weight back in the saddle. In extreme situations you can even drop your butt down behind your saddle to keep that center of gravity low.

• Use your brakes wisely. Too much front brake and you will fly over the front tire. Too much rear brake and you will skid. The best thing to do is feather the brakes to avoid losing control. Unfortunately, this one is mainly trial by fire.

Getting Over Stuff

Mountain bike trails are full of obstacles. It's really a cool feeling to get your bike up and over something you never thought you could. The basic skill you need to master to be able to do this is the wheelie.

• Approach the object with your weight centered over the bike, crank arms parallel to the ground, butt a few inches off the saddle, and arms and legs slightly bent. You're ready to take on that big ole log in the trail.

• Press down on the front handlebars. This compresses the tire. Then, shift your weight back. The tire will automatically come off the ground. At the same time, pull your arms up and back towards your chest to lift the front wheel even higher. You just popped a wheelie. You can also hammer down on the crank for a little extra whoomph.

• Once the front of your bike clears the object, shift your weight back to the neutral starting position to bring the rear tire over. Bring on the next rock.

Getting Through Water

Many of the trails in this book involve creek crossings. Creek crossings are good. They can be refreshing on a hot day and offer a fun challenge. You feel like a dork getting stuck in the middle, however, when your friends all go buzzing by throwing wakes that shimmer in the sun. Here's how to make sure you're the one leaving rainbows.

• Check out the bottom before you cross and look for the smoothest route. You won't make it across if you hit a boulder or drop into a swimming hole.

• Enter the water in a medium gear and keep pedaling until you get to the other side. Coasting and liquid don't mix.

ACCESS FOR ALL

TRAIL ETIQUETTE

We're beggin' you here to do your darndest to keep trails open to all fat tire fiends. The actions of a few have threatened access for the rest of us in a lot of parts of the country and it's starting to happen in Austin.

When we came out with the first edition of this book in 1993, trail closures were mainly an issue in California. They are now an issue in Central Texas.

We have had to take some locations out of this book over the years because they are no longer open to mountain biking. That number has really gone up in the last couple of years and is threatening some of our best in-town getaways.

The National Off-Road Bicycle Association has written a code that is imperative to obey. We cannot stress enough the importance of following this code whether you are a seasoned racer or a beginner to the sport. It is no exaggeration to say that if you break this code, you are putting the whole sport in danger. It sounds dramatic, but thems the facts.

NORBA CODE

1. I will yield the right of way to other non-motorized recreationists. I realize that people judge cyclists by my actions.

2. I will slow down and use caution when approaching or overtaking another and will make my presence known well in advance.

3. I will maintain control of my speed at all times and will approach turns in anticipation of someone around the bend.

4. I will stay on designated trails to avoid trampling native vegetation and will minimize potential erosion to trails by not using muddy trails or short cutting switchbacks.

5. I will not disturb wildlife or livestock.

6. I will not litter. I will pack out what I pack in, and I will pack out more than my share whenever possible. (In other words; don't mess with Texas)

7. I will respect public and private property, including trail use signs and no trespassing signs, and I will leave gates as I have found them.

8. I will always be self-sufficient, and my destination and travel speed will be determined by my ability, my equipment, the terrain, and the present and potential weather conditions.

9. I will not travel solo when bikepacking in remote areas. I will leave word of my destination and when I plan to return.

10. I will observe the practice of minimum impact bicycling by "taking only pictures and memories and leaving only waffle prints."

11. I will always wear a helmet whenever I ride.

We have a couple of other rules as well. Please leave the rebel yell at home so others can enjoy nature in solitude. Also, after a rain, wait at least 24 hours to ride and then call the contact number to make sure the trail is open.

Each of these rides has its own policies that you need to be familiar with and observe. The status of some trails may have changed since the writing of this book, so above anything else, obey signs.

GET INVOLVED

As grim as the picture sounds, there are some groups in the nation, Texas, and Austin that are working their tails off to help mountain bikers gain and keep access to public lands. They can always use your support in terms of both time and money.

Do you think trails stay in good shape through osmosis and good vibes? Guess again. In addition to lobbying parks and other areas for our access, these groups organize the trail maintenance days that keep our playgrounds looking good.

Please do your part by getting involved with one of the following groups:

IMBA

IMBA (International Mountain Biking Association) is a nonprofit group that represents people concerned with mountain biking issues. That's us. Their mission is "to promote mountain biking opportunities through environmentally and socially responsible use of the land."

They:

• Distribute info about safe, minimal impact riding

• Publish a newsletter about mountain bike access issues

• Help form local mountain bike clubs

• Provide educational material

• Work with other organizations to help get more public lands and open those lands to mountain bike use

Basically they are working hard to assure multiple use of trails. The only way for that to happen is for all mountain bikers to be educated and responsible. By using rules such as the NORBA code, bikers can show that we are legitimate users that cause minimal trail impact. The biggest thing you can do to help out is ride responsibly and respect existing policies.

Find out about joining IMBA by writing them at: IMBA PO Box 7578, Boulder, CO 80306. You can also find out about all they do on their website at www.imba.com.

Texas Bicycle Coalition

Another great group is the TBC. They act as the voice of bikers in Texas state politics. They address both on and off road issues. Most importantly for fat tire followers is the fact that the TBC is a consultant to the Texas Parks & Wildlife department for off road trails in state parks.

They are also kind of a clearing house for information on what's happening in the state in terms of biking events. Their website, www.biketexas.org, is a cornucopia of biking info. Races, centuries, fun rides, and any other biking event in the state are listed. Check it out.

By joining the TBC you can help insure the protection of cyclist rights, know that you are represented before state policy makers, and receive a newsletter on biking issues and programs around the state.

Contact them at: PO Box 1121, Austin, TX 78767. (512) 476-7433. (bikemail@biketexas.org)

Austin Ridge Riders

You know that bumper sticker that says "Think globally, Act locally"? The Ridge Riders is your chance to act locally as they are the IMBA affiliate club for Austin. (You also get a discount on IMBA dues if you're a member of the Ridge Riders.)

The Ridge Rider's focus is community trail development and maintenance. That's YOUR community hoss. They also do fun stuff like organize group rides for all levels of riders and have a social hour (a.k.a. happy hour) once a month.

People new to the sport can learn loads at their beginner clinics where they go over bike handling skills, bike maintenance, and Martha Stewart proper trail etiquette.

If you feel your competitive juices flowing and want to race, the Ridge Riders sponsor races and even have their own team.

You can get the full scoop at www.io.com/austinridgeriders.

RACE FACE

Some people like the competition, others the party, others the swag (that means free stuff.) Whatever the reason, mountain bike races are pretty darn popular.

In Texas we have the Texas State Championship Series, which is a set of races all over the state. Riders get points according to how they place in their category. The categories are determined by sex, age, and riding ability. (You can earn extra points by doing trail work.) Your point total from eight races is combined, and if you have a high score you get to ride in the finals.

The events here are big fun. There are kids "races", group rides, rocking parties, and tons of cool people just hangin' out.

The Texas Mountain Bike Racing Association organizes and runs the series. If you want more info you can go to their website at www.tmbra.org.

SEND OFF

All right! Now we are ready to go. We are getting excited just thinking about the transformation that takes place as we hop on our bikes and leave work and pressures behind. We hope that you also catch the fever and get involved not only in riding, but also with the groups that are working to keep the trails open for all of us. Not all of us can bunny-hop up cliffs, but we can all pitch in the effort to sustain our sport.

EXTRA STUFF

We are always looking for new trails and helpful hints. We have forms in the back of this book that you can mail in if you have any suggestions for future printings or if you want to order more copies. You can also just write us to say, "*hola*" at:

Ragged Edge Riders
P.O. Box 161862
Austin, TX 78716
ragged-edge-riders@austin.rr.com

LAWYER SECTION - READ THIS

Mountain biking is an inherently dangerous venture (We have the scars to prove it if you want to see them). Even the most cautious riders risk hurting themselves (or worse) every time out. This book is not a substitute for good skills, judgement or topo maps. We are in no way responsible for any injury, property damage or violation of the law that may occur in connection with the use of this book. You are responsible for yourself.

Walnut Creek

Emma Long

Austin

Rides

Town Lake Hike-and-Bike
Easy

Start :   Austin High School
Length: 10 mile loop with smaller loops
Contact: Austin PARD (512) 499-6700
Website: www.ci.austin.tx.us/parks/metroparks.htm

The Town Lake trail is the queen of over 20 miles of hike and bike trails in Austin. This loop, an Austin tradition since 1978, hosts a daily mishmash of walkers, joggers, bikers and posers (our friend's mom even saw a streaker). The trail is usually crowded so remember the golden rule - - slow down in congested areas and alert people when you pass. Keep an eye out for the 3000 trees and shrubs, the special architecture, Lady Bird's wildflowers, Stevie Ray's Memorial and the huge bat sculpture.

Our favorite section is the loop between Austin High and Congress, including the "Bat Facts" area in front of the Four Seasons. To do the whole loop you have to ride on the sidewalk for a while and eat some exhaust, but you also have the reward of riding on less crowded sections of the trail. However you do it, we're sure you'll come away smiling.

After your ride, cool off in Barton Springs - Texas' most famous swimming hole. The pristine, almost holy waters are a MUST for the total Austin experience. For food and libations hit any of the spots along Barton Springs Road - Shady Grove has the best patio and Chuy's the best Tex-Mex.

0.0 - Cross over the MoPac footbridge and hang a left.
0.9 - Pass the gazebo at Lou Neff Point where Barton Creek flows into Town Lake; feed the ducks, or the swans if you're lucky, then take a left over the Barton Creek footbridge.
1.5 - You can take the high road here to start back on the smallest loop (2.9 miles) over the Lamar bridge, or continue on.
2.2 - After you pass the 1st Street gazebo and reflection pond at the official start of the trail, make another loop (4.1 miles) decision.
2.8 - Follow the bike lane to Riverside Drive and go left on Riverside's sidewalk for 1.3 miles.
4.1 - Take a left on Lake Shore Blvd where you will hook up with the trail.
4.4 - Take the left fork to continue around Town Lake on the main trail.
6.0 - After crossing Longhorn Dam, take a left and circle around the Holly Creek Power Plant.
8.0 - The trail splits; go left to stay on the Town Lake Trail.
10.1 - Wasn't that a kicker outing? Last one to Barton Springs is a rotten egg!

Town Lake Hike-and-Bike

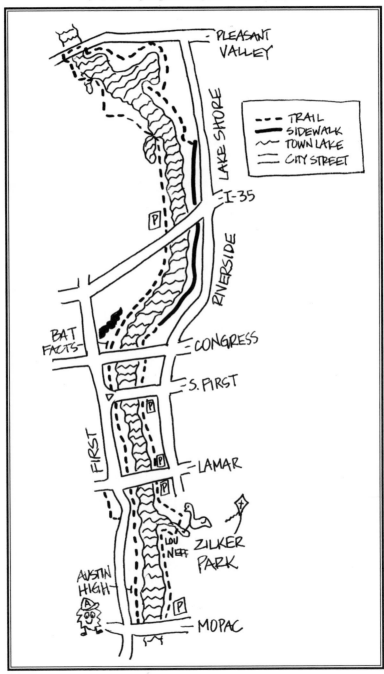

Shoal Creek Greenbelt
Easy

Start:	Any number of places along Lamar between 9th and 38th
Length:	3 miles one way
Contact:	Austin PARD (512) 499-6700
Website:	www.ci.austin.tx.us/parks/greenbelts.htm

This pleasant, shady trail is a less-traveled extension of the Town Lake Hike and Bike trail. Running along (and over and across) Shoal Creek, it is a nice casual ride that is fun to combine with a picnic or a game of frisbee golf.

This place has special significance for us because it was one of the first bike outings we ever took. Mom and Dad would pile the bikes in the station wagon and it would take us all day to go out and back (it requires a lot of time to ride, catch a minnow, ride, catch a crawdad, ride, swing, ride, climb a tree, ride, go the bathroom, ride...).

Because this ride is so pleasant, and is next to a residential part of town, there are usually walkers and joggers on the trail too. It's not as crowded as Town Lake, but you need to remember your etiquette. There's a pool at Pease Park for your summer time enjoyment and a number of eateries along Lamar. Try the Whole Foods Market at 6th and Lamar.

How to get there - The trail starts just east of 1st and Lamar, but there is trail damage due to flooding on some parts of it so we are going to start you at Duncan Park. From Austin High, take 1st street east to Lamar, go north on Lamar and then one block east on 9th where Duncan Park will be on the left. See the map for other points of trail access (there are tons).

0.0   Rev up the buggy and head north (right) on the trail; depending on the time of the year there may or may not be much water in the creek.
0.7   Hang a left over the bridge and ride through Pease Park - pick out a swing for the return trip.
1.8   The trail crosses the road, look for it on the other side.
2.0   River crossing here, so if it's high you're going to get wet; work on your boulder maneuvers or just walk the bike.
2.3   Now you've hit the low clearance area. This is our favorite part because we feel like we're spelunking or rock climbing.
2.4   The trail comes out here on 31st street, go left and ride in the bike lane for .1 miles until it hooks back up at Seider Spring Park where there was a massacre under the oaks in 1842.

Shoal Creek Greenbelt

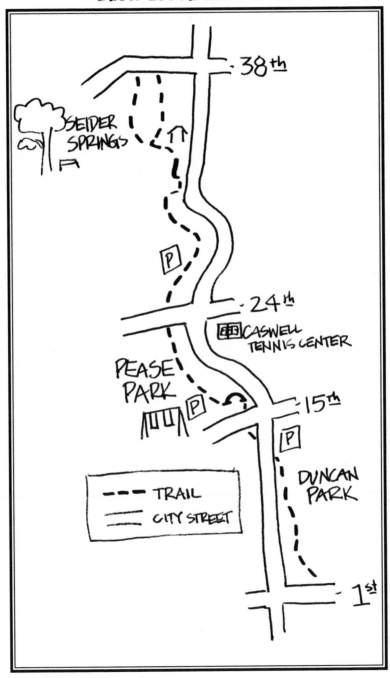

Mary Moore Searight Park
Easy

Start:	Off Slaughter Lane by I35
Length:	2 mile loop
Contact:	Austin PARD 499-6700
Website:	www.ci.austin.tx.us/parks/metroparks.htm

This "Zilker South" is a huge 344 acre park that is a well-kept secret from many people in Austin. Three cheers to Mary Moore Searight who turned down big bucks from developers to donate 206 acres of her land to the city. Now it's a cool place for an easy ride through the woods.

Thanks also to the Texas Parks and Wildlife Department for the $500,000 facilities grant. Not only does the park have a hike and bike trail, but it also has volleyball courts, tennis courts, basketball courts, a baseball field, a soccer field, a covered picnic area, a fishing pier, a Frisbee golf course and an equestrian trail. You can bring all your sports equipment and make a day of it here. We've come out with a bunch of friends and been "activity central" for a couple of multi-sport hours.

The trail itself it a nice, wide, caliche-covered swath through the Texas Hill Country. It crosses over the creek and meanders through the trees for an enjoyable but short two mile loop. You might be tempted to sashay off on to the horse trail, but DON'T. As with the other Austin parks, yield to everything that moves more slowly than you do.

The park is on the outskirts of town and we suggest taking a picnic for the best eats. Unfortunately there's no pool out there, but there's always Slaughter Creek.

How to get there - From Austin High take 1st street east to I-35. Turn right and take I-35 South about 7 miles to the W. Slaughter Lane exit. Take a right on Slaughter Lane and go down about 1.5 miles where you will see the entrance to the park on the left. Follow the road all the way down to the bottom parking lot. The bike trail is on the right. The park is open from 5 a.m. to 10 p.m.

This is another trail where no specific directions are needed because it is so well marked and there are no real decision points. Just head out there and play the day away.

Mary Moore Searight Park

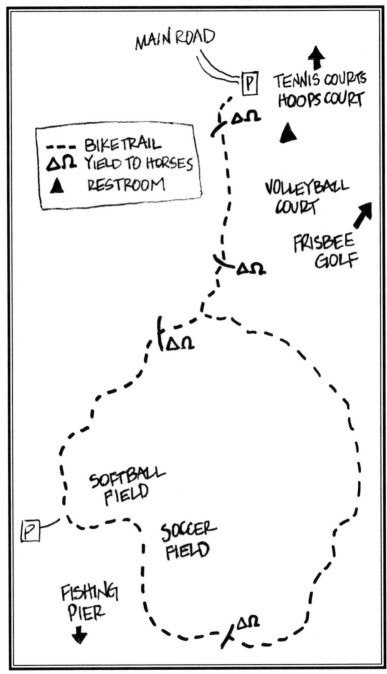

MAIN ROAD

P

TENNIS COURTS
HOOPS COURT

BIKE TRAIL
ΔΩ YIELD TO HORSES
▲ RESTROOM

VOLLEYBALL
COURT

FRISBEE
GOLF

SOFTBALL
FIELD

P

SOCCER
FIELD

FISHING
PIER

Bull Creek Greenbelt
Easy/Intermediate

Start:	Near RR2222 and 360
Length:	About 2.5 miles one way
Contact:	Austin PARD (512) 327-5437
Website:	www.ci.austin.tx.us/parks/greenbelts.htm

This trail is the perfect place for the beginner to get a little more adventuresome, or for the more advanced rider to have a nice, fast ride. This county park borders Bull Creek from RR2222 to Spicewood Springs Road and offers mostly unimproved double track trails with some great scenery. Following the creek on rock ledges, the trail leads you to waterfalls and still pools that make you happy you live in Austin.

There is a fun single track section from Laurel Wood to Loop 360. It goes through a little field and then drops down to the creek where you ride right along the edge until you cross under the 360 bridge. From there it turns to double track. This double track is a good starting place for the beginners wanting to test their skills. Stay along the creek and you'll come back around to Loop 360 again. This area has a bathroom, parking lot and good swimming hole.

Continue under 360 and you'll have a choice of riding along the west or east sides of the creek. The east side is much nicer and smoother than the west side, so cross the creek and follow the trail up to Spicewood Springs Rd.

Bikers have done some harm to the park so certain areas are off-limits. Pay attention to all signs and never, ever ride in closed areas. PARD is willing to work with us but we can't abuse our privileges.

Swimming is an option anywhere along the creek, but there is a good swimming hole, rope swing and waterfall marked on the map near the parking lot. There is also a good place to swim near Laurel Wood. Now that you are starving for some Tex-Mex, get back on 360 going towards 2222. After you cross the bridge, take a left at the light onto Westlake Dr and turn left into Davenport Village. Some of the best rita's and cheese enchiladas await you at Maudie's Milagro.

How to get there - You can access the trail in a number of places. We like to start where Laurel Wood dead ends in the trail, but there is no good parking there. For the best parking, take MoPac north to RR2222. From 2222 take a right onto Loop 360 north; after the first light go .4 miles further and take a left onto the paved road. This road leads around to the parking lot, which is the one noted on the map.

Bull Creek Greenbelt

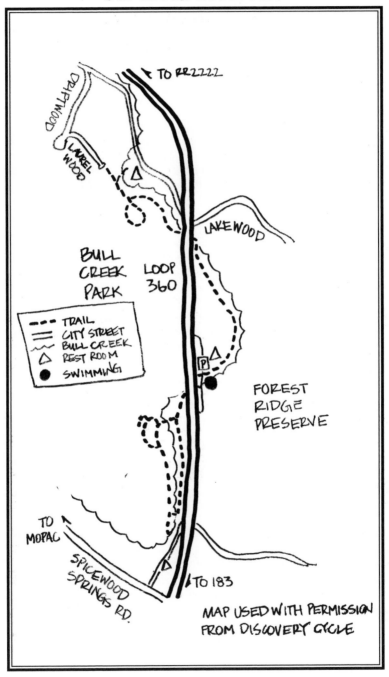

McKinney Falls State Park
Easy/Intermediate

Start :   At falls, open 8am to 10pm every day
Length: 3 miles
Contact: (512) 243-1643
Website: www.tpwd.state.tx.us/park/mckinney

This mesquite umbrella-ed single track is a trip for any level rider and McKinney is just a nice place to be. The terrain is very smooth with virtually no rocks or hills and the trail is nice and twisty but not too tight. You can stay seated the majority of the ride and crank around in your middle ring with only your skills and tires forcing you to hit the breaks.

This is a great place to take a beginner because it is so smooth and flat and there are jeep trails to escape on if needed. It is also *padre* for the more seasoned shredder to see how far over your bike can be leaned before entering that fabulous razor-thin zone between having traction and beefing (falling over.) Along the way make sure you check out the McKinney homestead and the gristmill.

To get to the trailhead cross the creek above the falls, take the jeep road towards the McKinney homestead and take a left at the Homestead trail sign. Be CAREFUL when crossing the creek to get to the trailhead because it is very slippery. Also be sure you have your patch kit with you because of mesquite thorns.

After you're done riding, go down to the falls and swim in one of the local legends. This is a great place to pass a long, hot day. (Watch out for skipping rocks.)

For nourishment you have to stop at El Azteca on the way back into Austin. It's at 2600 East 7th about a mile and a half before you cross under IH35. This Austin tradition has been in business over 30 years and has succulent cabrito and no *cabrones*.

How to get there - McKinney is about 13 miles from Austin High and it takes about 25 minutes to get there. From Austin High take 1st street (Caesar Chavez) east and go under I-35. Turn left (north) on the access road and take it to 7th street. Turn right on 7th street and follow the signs to 183 south toward Lockhart. Take 183S to Scenic Loop Road, which is at a stop light. Go right on Scenic Loop Road until it dead ends at McKinney Falls Parkway. Go right and the entrance is .5 miles down on the left. The price is $2 per person 13 or older.

McKinney Falls State Park

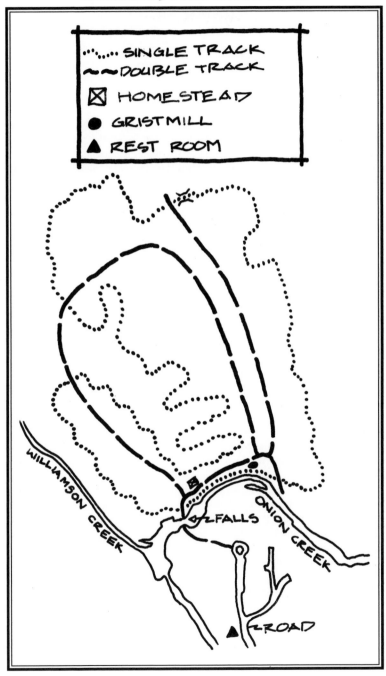

Barton Creek Greenbelt
Intermediate

Start:	Barton Springs or Loop 360 near MoPac
Length:	7.7 miles one way (intermediate)
Contact:	Austin PARD (512) 478-0905; Hotline 472-1267
Website:	www.ci.austin.tx.us/parks/greenbelts.htm

This trail is the heart, the soul, the grand poobah, the source, the primal origin (you get the picture) of mountain biking in Austin. From the rider just starting to shred the single track to the John Tomac (that's an old reference, isn't it?) expert, there's fun for everyone along the Barton Greenbelt.

These relatively smooth, packed-dirt single track trails are a joy to ride and the scenery along the creek is spectacular. This, along with its central location, make it one of the most crowded trails in Austin however, so watch for hikers, kids, dogs and riders slower than yourself. Be especially careful in the stretch from Barton Springs to Loop 360, as it's rocky and highly traveled.

Mountain bikes are IN DANGER OF LOSING ACCESS to this trail so yield to everyone and never ride on closed trails. Follow the NORBA code or else we may not be able to ride out here much longer.

There are a couple of swimming holes along the trail, but Barton Springs is a must if you have never been there. The **Town Lake Hike-and-Bike** write-up has the scoop on swimming and eating in this area.

How to get there - There are a few places to access the trail, but the most popular one is at Barton Springs. From Austin High, take 1st Street east to Lamar and then Lamar south over the river. Hang a right on Barton Springs road and then a left into Zilker Park. The trail head is past the pool and concessions at Barton Springs. Another good access point is on Loop 360: take MoPac south to 360 East, take a left at the first light and then a left into the parking lot; go straight to the greenbelt parking area.
This mileage assumes you're starting at Barton Springs:

1.6	First creek crossing; follow green and white arrows for bikes
1.8	Second creek crossing; cross chicken wire dam and go left
3.3	Creek crossing
3.6	Cross gully and follow signs
4.5	Cross if you can; if not, go straight and port bike using chain
4.7	Creek crossing
5.3	Creek crossing; cross and go left
7.3	Climb the Hill of Life; almost half a mile and 300' climb

Barton Creek Greenbelt

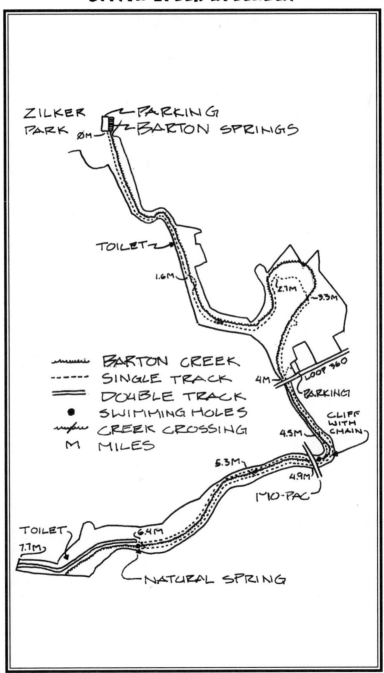

Muleshoe Bend
Easy/Intermediate

Start:	Muleshoe Recreation Area, Lake Travis
Length:	7.5 miles
Contact:	(512) 473-4083
Website:	www.lcra.org/lands/muleshoe.html

This great single track loop is located in a 1,000 acre park with several miles of Lake Travis shoreline. Wildlife abounds. The trail is the result of efforts by the Austin Ridge Riders, who deserve commendation for an excellent job. The loop is directional, so make sure you are going the right way and be sure to yield at the multiple jeep road crossings.

For the most part this trail is void of rocks and it has minimal climbing. It does have a few short technical sections, but you can sit, spin, lean and grin on most of it. The majority of the loop is under the cover of trees, which provide for the ultimate in tight single track action. The trail follows the natural terrain, changing from light soil and mesquites on the flats to dark soil and cedars on the hillsides.

This is a great place to work on your handling skills as the trail is constantly twisting through the white shine oaks and Mexican tea leaves. The chances of getting lost are very slim because this is the only trail and the road crossings are well marked. On warm days you can always squeeze a couple of extra miles out knowing that the clear waters of Lake Travis are waiting for you when you bonk.

After the water has given you back enough energy to drive, head for the best Mexican chow around. Rosie's Tamale House is right before you get the intersection of 620 and HWY 71 on the left. There is a Rosie's To Go on the right, but you need to get the full experience and see the photos at the sit down. If you are craving a brew dog, go to a convenience store at 620 and 71 and stock up. Rosie doesn't sell it, but she'll let you bring it in.

How to get there - This 32 mile trip takes less than 45 minutes and is fairly easy to find. Take MoPac South to Southwest Parkway and head West on Highway 71. After you cross the Pedernales, go a little less than 2 miles and take a right on Pale Face Ranch Road/404. Go 4.5 miles and take a right on 414 at the Windermere sign. Go 2.5 miles on 414 (veer right at the entrance to Ridge Harbor) and you will be at the park. If you don't want to swim you can park in the lot on the left and the trail is right there. If you do want to swim, go down the dirt road, take a right at the Y on Trammel and park down by the lake. The park is open 24 hours a day and costs $5 per car per day.

Muleshoe Bend

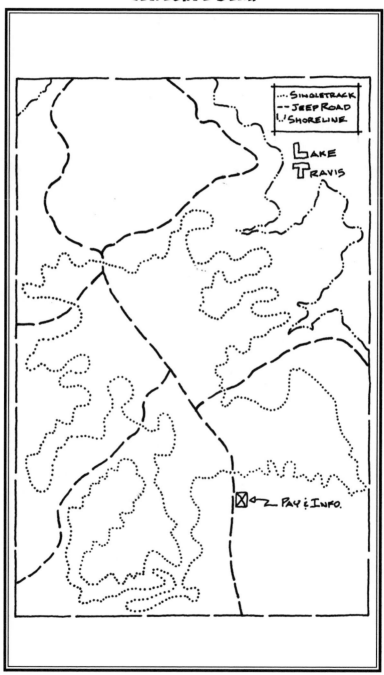

Walnut Creek Greenbelt
Easy/Intermediate

Start:	Near the swimming pool
Length:	It's a maze of trails
Contact:	Austin PARD (512) 327-5437
Website:	www.ci.austin.tx.us/parks/greenbelts.htm

This 516 acre park with lots of smooth single track is a blast to ride and is a nice change of pace compared to most of the rocky terrain around Austin. Its in lowlands and has numerous creeks on it. Its a great place for a beginner to learn the world of dirt but it also will challenge the more experienced with tight and twisty single track, jumps and some quick drops. The evaluation change is fairly mellow and some of the climbs are short and steep.

This trail system can be ridden with two different points of view, a giant mellow BMX park or a cross county course. There are some great whoop-de-doo sections that you will want to do more than once and some good jumps to session on. Most of the single track is tight and built so that you can get a great flow going as you slalom through the trees. Practice jamming some sections at 100% then do it again. Even the jeep roads are fun because you can carry a lot of speed on most of them.

A few notes of caution about riding here. One is that sometimes there are a lot of people walking with dogs, particularly on the trails near the pool. Please be cautious, slow down, and say hi to everyone. We don't want to loose this jewel. The other is the fact that it's truly a maze of trails and it is easy to get disoriented. Half the fun is learning the trails so be sure and use the power lines as a point of reference. The good thing is that if you get a little backwards, you are never far from streets or the parking lot. The last note is that the creek crossing can be very slippery so be prepared.

After putting the hammer down for the last time, the pool is right there and opens during the summer. Now that you're tired and refreshed, its time to scarf. Go back the way you came and take a right off of Parmer into the center with the Randals. Chipolte Mexican Grill is your destination. Order up some giant burritos, a few cold ones and plan your next ride.

How to get there – Take MoPac North and exit Parmer which is the last exit before the traffic lights start . Go right on Parmer for 1.5 miles. Take a right on Loop 275 South (Lamar) and go 0.5 miles. The entrance is on your right. After you cross the bridge, take a left into the parking lot by the pool. The ride is free.

Thanks to Josh Karnes and crew for the great map.

Walnut Creek Greenbelt

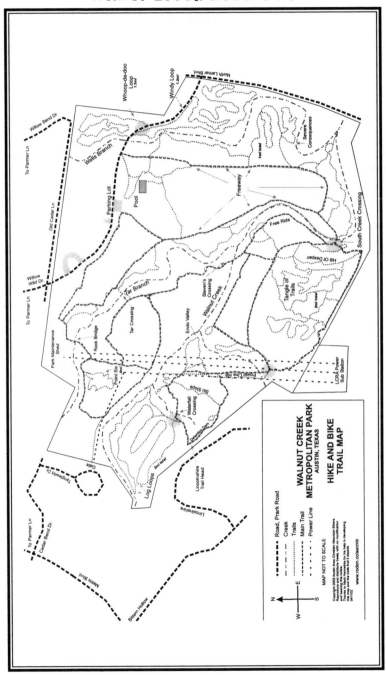

WALNUT CREEK
METROPOLITAN PARK
AUSTIN, TEXAS

HIKE AND BIKE
TRAIL MAP

MAP NOT TO SCALE

Road, Prark Road
Creek
Trails
Main Trail
Power Line

Copyright 2002 Austin Area Christian Mountain Bikers.
Reproduce and distribute freely with no modification
and bearing this notice.
Thanks to Mark Hanneke for his help in developing
this map and the trails that it depicts.
041102

www.roden.cc/aacmb

Emma Long Motocross Park
Difficult

Start: Oak Shore Drive out by Lake Austin and City Park
Length: 6 mile main loop
Contact: Austin PARD (512) 837-4500
Website: www.ci.austin.tx.us/parks/metroparks.htm

Put on your technical helmet and an old big ring if you have never ridden this loop before. With race names such as *Gluttons for Punishment*, this loop is not for the weak of heart (nor is it a good place to learn how to use your new clipless pedals).

The main 6 mile loop is a blast and has about 110 feet of climbing with enough short technical rock sections to please even the most demanding techno-addicts. The loop runs one way, which is clearly marked at the trailhead. There are also signs along the route.

The trails are 99% single track with a mixture of a few smooth sections and a lot of rocky parts that twist tightly through the cedars. Be prepared to have to dismount a few times on your first ride, but these sections will keep you awake at night and coming back for more. The trails were originally for motorcycles, which can still be ridden out here, so be aware of them (Peace on dirt). Once you get a good flow going, lactic acid and rock ledges are your only obstacles. The course may seem short in length but it will take longer than you think and, we guarantee, is more fun every time you ride it.

Along the way you will have seen signs telling you not to change the course. Pay attention to them. This area is an endangered species habitat (Golden Warbler) and making new trails is against the law.

After you ride, head to Ski Shores for a dip in the lake, a great burger and a coldie. To get there, take a left out of the parking lot and go .2 miles on Oak Shore Road. Take a right on Pierce and go .6 miles down the hill to Ski Shores (be sure to try the stuffed jalapeños). Hang out, listen to acoustic guitar, enjoy the breeze off the lake and think how lucky you are to live in Austin.

How to get there - Take MoPac north to the RR2222 exit. Go left on Northland and then right on 2222 4.5 miles to the light at City Park Road. Turn left (the only way you can go) and take City Park Road 3.8 miles (staying right at the fork) to Oak Shore Road. Take a left on Oak Shore and continue .9 miles until you see the Emma Long Motocross sign on the left.

Emma Long Motocross Park

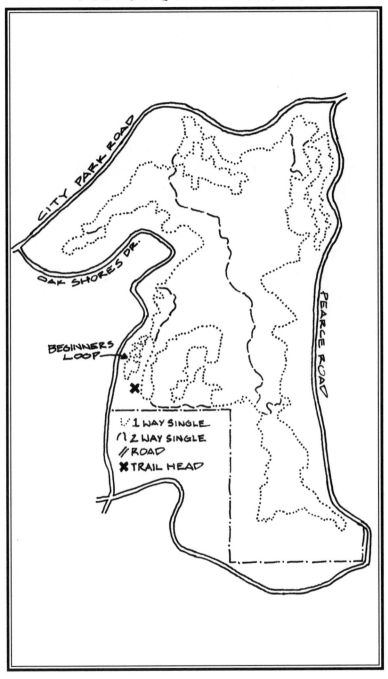

EMMA LONG

Day Trip

Rides

Colorado Bend State Park
All Levels

Start: On Colorado River; closed in Dec-Jan
Length: 15 miles of trails
Contact: (915) 628-3240
Website: www.tpwd.state.tx.us/park/colorado/

These little known trails on the banks of our Colorado River are a real find. You can do everything here from hiking to biking to even spelunking. The bike trails can be broken down into three different sections for different levels of riders.

The network of 5.7 miles of jeep roads and single track trails up top is for intermediate/advanced riders. The paths are rocky and rough in some sections with gently climbing hills. The jeep trails are like double single track and can really be shredded on the downhills. Another section is the smooth dirt road (the same one that you drive on), which is about 6 miles long with 400 feet of elevation change. It is also intermediate/advanced because of the climb and the need to watch for cars.

The 3.3 miles down by the river is a gratifying beginner/intermediate section because it is fairly smooth and flat. This section offers some welcome shade along with pleasant views of the river and lots of places to swim. For a real workout there is a great 30 mile ride to be had here. You can park by the river, ride up the dirt road to the trails up top, take the river trail upstream and then back-track all the way to the spring.

By far the best place for a dip after this long ride is the spring at the north end of the river trail. This oasis provides cool, clear water in a beautiful surrounding that will keep that silly grin on your face for a while.

On your way back you can't miss Storm's Drive-In on the left as you pass through Lampasas. You can get a great burger and watch the locals cruise the joint.

How to get there - This trip is 90 miles and takes just over 2 hours. Take MoPac north and exit onto 183 north. Stay on 183N all the way to Lampasas. Go through a few lights and there will be signs for both 580 and the park. Go left on 580 for 21 miles until the road dead ends. Take a left, which turns into a dirt road, and follow the signs to the park headquarters about 9 more miles to pay your $3. CALL FIRST to make sure they are open.

Colorado Bend State Park

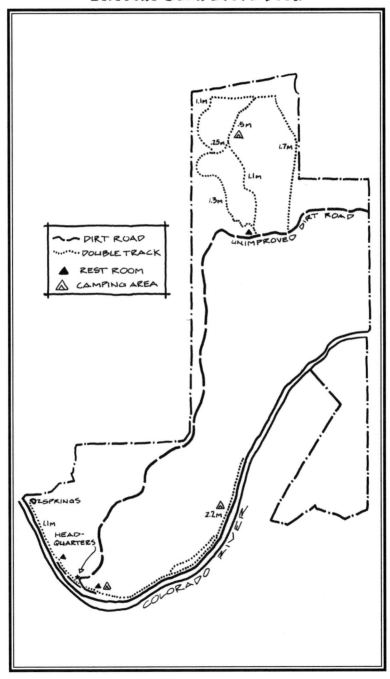

DIRT ROAD
DOUBLE TRACK
▲ REST ROOM
⛺ CAMPING AREA

Rocky Hill Ranch
All Levels

Start:	By Bastrop, TX; open 9am-dark daily
Length:	What ever you want (tons of trails)
Contact:	Grey Hill (512) 237-3112
Website:	www.rockyhillranch.com

Texas has cattle ranches, sheep ranches, wild game ranches and is now starting to get some mountain bike ranches. Rocky Hill is a great one that should definitely be on your weekend or afternoon-off agenda. Located near Bastrop in the Lost Pines area, Rocky Hill offers a complete change of scenery less than an hour from Austin.

The ranch has something for every level of rider so it might be fun to take a group. It ranks its trails like ski runs with green ones for beginners, blue trails for intermediates and black for advanced. The green trails are mostly scenic double track roads with occasional single track meandering through meadows. The blues are rollicking single track through the trees that make you feel like you've entered the free-play zone. And then there are the blacks. Tight, twisty, turny delight under a fragrant pine canopy with creek crossings and some good uphill grunts make the blacks fat tire heaven.

You really get your $6 worth at Rocky Hill. Not only are the trails very well marked, but also there are water stations along some of the trails. In addition, there is a double downhill slalom course for you and your buddies to determine who has bragging rights.

After the ride you can sit in bliss in the covered restaurant and enjoy a black bean burrito and some cold Shiner Bock. The restaurant, built completely from wood off the ranch, has such an inviting allure that you may want to hang out all evening and to camp out at the Rocky Hill camp sites or down the road at Buescher State Park.

How to get there - This trip is about 39 miles and takes less than an hour. From Austin High take 1st street east to I-35. Turn left (north) on the access road and take it to 7th street. Turn right on 7th veering left to Hwy 71 East after you cross the Colorado River. Go through Bastrop and take the Smithville exit about 11 miles down the road. Go left on FM153 East 2.3 miles and you will see the old bike on the pine gate entrance on the left. We always have to mention our favorite trails:
E/Z Pickens - intermediate; twisty turny fun through the pines
Off the Lip - difficult; tightest trail here; not for the broad of butt
Rocky Hill - difficult; tough trail that takes no prisoners

Rocky Hill Ranch

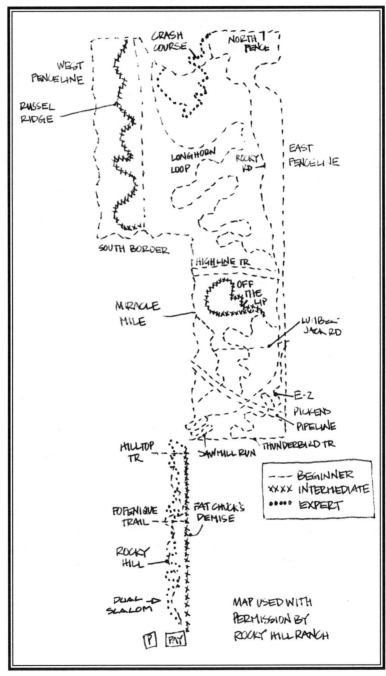

Hill Country State Natural Area
All Levels

Start: Outside of Bandera, TX; CALL FIRST
Length: 32 miles of trails (all levels)
Contact: Hill Country State Natural Area (830) 796-4413
Website: www.tpwd.state.tx.us/park/hillcoun/hillcoun.htm

This day trip offers an excellent taste of the Texas hill country with a wide variety of terrain and a mixture of single track and old jeep trails. Hillier than Austin, Bandera means some longer climbs than we can get at home which in turn means some lubed downhill rewards. Moco miles of well-marked trails, an excellent swimming hole and some of the best enchiladas in the state will send you home from this day radiating good karma.

Head back to town and take a left after you cross the bridge for a cool, clear swim in the Medina River. Dry off and continue down Main Street for dinner at El Jacalito, taking a left on Cedar and another left on 11th. Order the Jacalito special and send someone across the street to bring back beers from Domingos 11th Street Bar – you'll be in a state of bliss.

How to get there - (2 hours, 115 miles) 1st street east to I35 south; exit I35 near New Braunfels on 46 West to Boerne and Bandera; In Bandera take 173 south to a quick right on 1077 west which turns to dirt after about 5 miles; follow signs to the office to pay your $3/person.

Bandera is the heart of Dude Ranch country so remember that bikes ALWAYS yield to horses. Stick to the double track lower elevations trails for easier rides (#s 8,9,1 and 6) or pick out a killer loop with lots of single track and hills for a difficult grunt. The following are our favorite loops.

The Trip to the Top - (8.8 miles, difficult) This loop is guaranteed to get your heart pumping from both exertion and adrenaline. There are two major climbs, fast downhills, and some proper single track sections. Take #2 to #3, go right on #3A for technical single track and a 300 foot climb that may include pushing the bike, go right on #3 to sneak up on the codger at the Hermit's Shack, come back over until you hit #4, hammer to the top on #4A and enjoy the view of Cougar Canyon while you try to get your lungs back in order, bonzai back down #4A, right on #4 and its downhill all the way home.

Single Track Sashay - (5.1 miles, intermediate) Single track heaven with some good technical sections and creek crossings. From #1, right on #5A for a little climb, left on #6 for a fast, fun section, left on #6A, and right on #7 for some tight turns and water play.

Hill Country State Natural Area

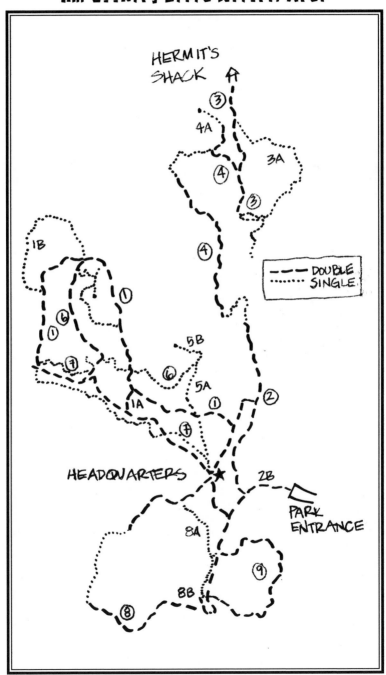

BLORA/Trailblazer Mt Bike Park
All Levels

Start: Parking lot of the bike park, near Belton
Length: 8.5 mile intermediate/difficult loop; 4 mile beginner loop
Contact: BLORA Administrative Office; (254) 287-4907
Website: www.hoodmrw.com/blora.htm

With lots of single track, a good amount of elevation change and some very challenging sections this trail should not be missed. Pay your money, slap on a grin and get readyyyyyy to rummmmble! Pick up a map at the trail head and follow the letters to the well marked route of your choice. The 8.5 mile loop is 99% single track and throws a little of everything at you. The first section is some great single that twists through the woods without much elevation change. A couple of miles into it, you have the option of keeping it at the beginner level by looping back around to the parking lot.

If you choose to continue, the fun has only begun. Liberty Downhill will set you free as you switchback across the hillside. We highly recommend taking Sparta Valley Ride Trail for some good climbs combined with two very sweet, banked, sweeping left hand turns. See how high you can take the high line or loft one near the apex. From here you will slap it into the big ring and stomp down to the lake. Enjoy the short flat section because the next .9 miles will test your soul. This climb takes you up the Devils Back Bone only to drop back down some before the final push up BLORA Bluff Trail. Keep pushing that granny and you might clean it. Either way once you get to the top you are rewarded with a view that make you forget what your legs feel like and remember what living is.

The best place to cool off is that great big lake you were looking at while your head was spinning after the climb. Go back to the BLORA Administration Office, cough up $3 and head down to the lake. Calorie replenishment will be key after BLORA Bluff, so head to Franks Lakeview Inn & Anchor Club to grab a table on the deck overlooking the lake. You can't go wrong with the burgers and fried green tomatoes. To get there, head back the way you came on Sparta but take a left at the stop sign on F.M. 439. After about 2.2 miles Franks will be on your left. If you pass the dam you've gone too far.

How to get there - This trip is about 55 miles and takes about 1.5 hours. Head North on Mo-Pac until you hit I-35. Take I-35 North to the Loop 121/exit 292 outside of Belton. Take Loop 121 West and after you cross the train tracks start looking for Sparta Road. It's about 4 miles total on Loop 121. Take a left on Sparta and go 8.2 miles. Go right at the BLORA entrance, past the mountain bike park on your left, to the Administration Office. Pay $6 and get your pass. The park is open dawn to 10pm daily.

BLORA/Trailblazer Mountain Bike Park

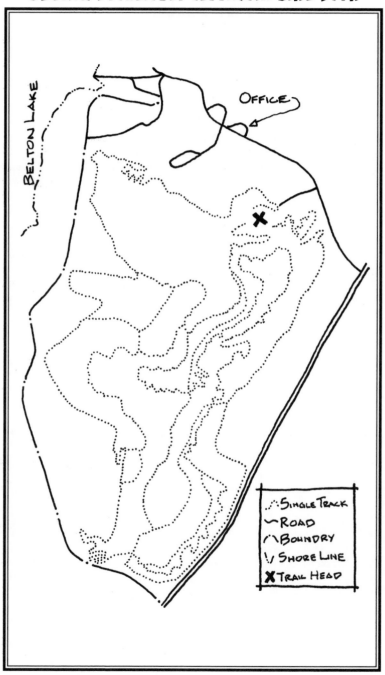

BELTON LAKE

OFFICE

X

Legend:
- Single Track
- Road
- Boundry
- Shore Line
- X Trail Head

Good Water Trail
All Levels

Start:	Georgetown Lake near Georgetown
Length:	6.6 miles one way
Contact:	Georgetown Lake HQ; (512) 930-5253
Website:	http://swf67.swf-wc.usace.army.mil/georgetown.gthiking.htm

This ride has two very different personalities, so where you start determines your fate. The signs at the park are not current. You ARE allowed to bike on the north side of the lake, but everything on the south side is hiking only. If you start at Russell Park you are forced to ride the difficult section, a mile long, rocky, single track decent. If this is your game, you will dig it here. The trail wanders through patches of large rocks that are like riding over a huge cheese grater. The rocks are sharp, require some commitment and have a mind of their own. From there the trail goes through the cedars to offer some nice views of the lake. It then drops down to the lake where a mixture of Jeep roads and single track run to Tejas. At one point the jeep road hits a small finger of the lake that floods the road sometimes. Even if its not flooded, we recommend taking the single track that goes to Walnut Springs Camp and around. The rest of the ride rolls through bottomland with well-marked single track sections.

If you park at Tejas Camp you can choose your level of difficulty. For an easy ride, just stay on the Jeep road. For an intermediate one, take all the single track sections. For a difficult ride, take the Jeep road until it ends, go left on the single track, rocky climb to the top and drop back down.

Where you park makes a difference in terms of swimming. If you want to ride the difficult section, we recommend parking at the "Beach". This way when you finish your ride, you are right there. Swimming from Tejas is more like swimming on the San Gabriel river, and is very pretty. Chow time will be at El Charrito. Drive back across I-35 and take a right on Austin Ave. Tacos & mole enchiladas are 0.5 miles down on the right. BYOB is the norm.

How to get there - These are both 45 minute drives. **Russell Park** - Take Mo-Pac north to I-35. Go north on I-35 to the Andis/Lake Georgetown exit. Go left on 2338 for about 6 miles and take a left on 3405 West. After a mile take a left on Russell Park Rd/262. To get to the trail head, take a right before the guard post to the parking lot. To get to the Beach, go through the guard post, park, and ride back up to the trail head. **Tejas Camp** - Take Mo-Pac to 183 and go north for 20 miles to Seward Junction(183 & 29). Go 0.75 miles past the Junction, take a right on 258 for 5.5 miles and the parking lot will be on your right. Unload and ride across the river on 258. The trail head is on the right. Entrance is free and the park is open daily from 6am – dark.

Good Water Trail

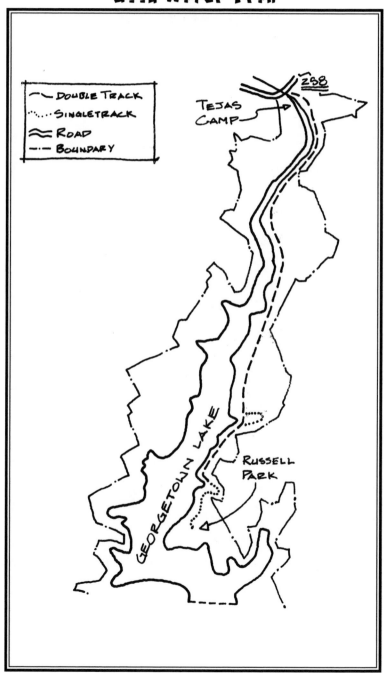

McAllister Park
Easy/Intermediate

Start:	2nd stop sign by Optimist Club sign, San Antonio
Length:	About 20 miles
Contact:	San Antonio PARD, (210) 821-3100
Website:	www.ci.sat.tx.us/sapar/

This 856 acre, relatively flat park is full of great twisting single track. One year it was rated one of the top 100 trails in the country! Don't worry, there are lots of bail-out points if you don't want to ride all 20 miles. The main loop, a mixture of single and double track, goes around the park. It is shown on the map. There is also a maze of more single track, all accessible from this loop. Most of this single track will eventually hit the loop again so go explore. Since this is a flat area with a creek, you should not ride after a rain.

If you take the trail head by the 2nd stop sign (Buckhorn Road and Leaping Fawn) you will hit the loop at a big rock. To get on the loop, go left or right. If you go straight, you hit the Mud Creek section, which is full of great tight single track through the trees that criss-crosses the creek. Don't worry about getting lost since this finger of the park is not that big. Just Zen out, swing the bike and take whichever trail your impulses desire. There is also a small open section that has some good jumps and berms to test your air time.

If you go right at the rock on the main loop you will eventually hit some fast Jeep roads by the baseball fields. This will drop you back down to Mud Creek on some good single track, splitting the oaks and yuccas. As the loop takes you back toward the park entrance it open ups some through the mesquites. After you cross the entrance road, the trail runs along the perimeter of the park and comes back to the big rock.

For grub, take a right out of the park on Jones Maltsberger. After 1.5 miles you will hit Thousand Oaks. There are lots of restaurants near this intersection. Go right on Thousand Oaks for two good choices. Pizza Italy has good pizza and the god of beers, Fat Tire Ale. Jack's, next door, has outdoor seating for good weather. See the O.P. Schanbel write-up for swimming.

How to get there - This trip is about 75 miles and will take at least an hour and 15 minutes depending on the traffic. Take I-35 South about 65 miles to 410 West. Take 410 W 5 miles to the 281 North exit. (San Pedro takes you to the 281 N entrance on the way out.) Go 2 miles on 281 N to the Bitters exit. Take a right on Bitters Road, which turns into Starcrest, for a mile to Jones Maltsberger. Take a left on Jones Maltsberger and the entrance to the park is about a mile on your right.

McAllister Park

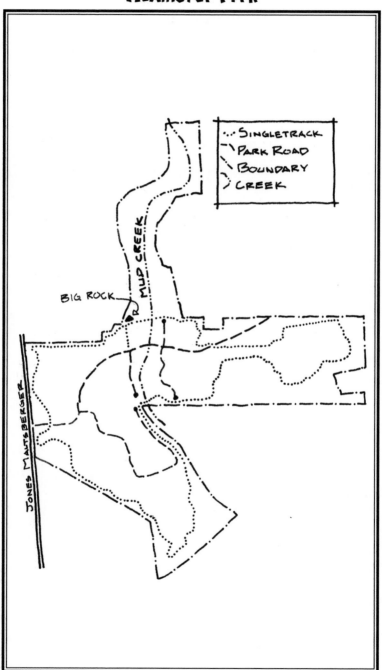

O.P. Schnabel Park
Easy/Intermediate

Start: Graff Pavilion in O.P. Schnabel Park, San Antonio
Length: 5 miles
Contact: San Antonio PARD, (210) 821-3000
Website: www.ci.sat.tx.us/sapar/

This ride is short but sweet. It's not long enough to warrant a road trip, but if you live by S.A., or are going to be there anyway, it's a fun pedal.

The map only shows the main trails. There is a maze of trails between the parking lot and the edge of the ridge. This flat section offers some tight single track under the canopy of the trees. When you are ready to take the short drop down to Leon Creek, there are over a half dozen ways to get down. The closer you are to the pavilion near the edge of the ridge, the harder they are. Some of these are extremely technical and should be walked before-hand. The easiest way to get down is to take a right at the pavilion, go straight where the hike & bike trail turns to the right, and take the trail closest to the red roofed house.

The single track trails on the ridge side of the creek are nice and smooth. There is a large section of rock in the creek bed where the main trail cuts the creek, which is a fun area to test your trials skills. Some of the trails on the golf course side of the creek have stretches of loose rocks that require high rpms and the ability to let your bike decide where it wants to go some of the time. Even though the trails in the park are limited, you can make up tiring loops by including the ridge top area.

After you are worn out, load up the rig and go back the way you came on 16. Go little over 1.5 miles and Grady's BBQ will be on your right. The building was built in 1946 and was originally a dance hall, but now serves brisket so tender you can cut it with a fork. Along with a full Q menu they also have some great fried catfish. The servings are generous and there is plenty of cold beer to help wash it down. For some of the clearest spring waters in Central Texas, get back on I-35N for 20 miles to Exit 187 (Seguin Avenue) in New Braunfels. Take a left on Seguin, go around the round-a-bout in historic down town, and the entrance to Landa Park will be a short ways down on your right. Park near the Aquatic Complex, slap down 4 bills, and go rejuvenate yourself in the cool (72 degree) crystal clear waters of the Comal river.

How to get there - This trip takes 1.5 hours and is about 80 miles. Take I-35 S 65 miles to 410W. Go on 410W 12 miles and take Exit 13A to 16 North(Bandera Road). Go 4 miles on 16 N and the park entrance will be on your right. Take a left where the road T's and park next to Graff Pavilion.

O.P. Schnabel Park

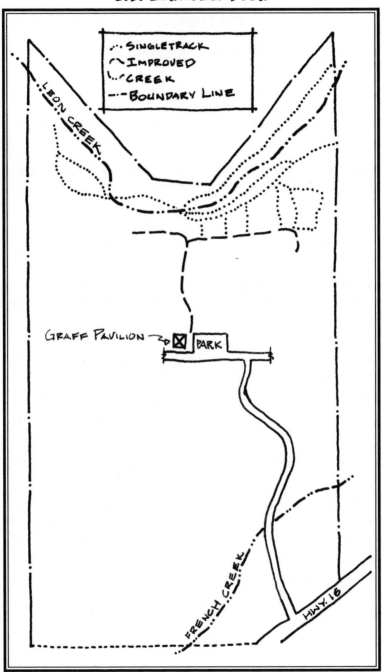

Pedernales Falls State Park
Intermediate

Start: Out 290 West toward Johnson City
Length: 7.5 mile loop
Contact: Pedernales Falls State Park (830) 868-7304
Website: www.tpwd.state.tx.us/park/pedernal

This is a relatively short and fast ride that is very fun in spite of being pretty easy. Set in the purple peaks of the Hill Country, Pedernales is a must see even for non-bikers. There are hiking trails, water falls and a great swimming area. When the water is up you can even go tubing. Every level of rider will be stoked after a day in this park.

The trail itself is mostly caliche-covered double track that winds down to the river. It crosses several streams and has both some uphill and downhill sections, none of which are too extreme but all of which are fast. The trail winds around enough to keep you honest on the downhills, which adds to the fun. Once the trail gets down to the river there is a single track section that snakes through the trees back up Wolf Mountain. burly fun going either up or down. This comes out onto a double track ridge going around both sides of the hill with some spectacular views.

This ride is great for beginner/intermediates ready to make that next step and test their mettle on single track because the single track portion is short and manageable. True beginners could just go out and back (skipping the single track) and still enjoy a nice ride. Advanced riders can really smoke it and go for oxygen debt and lactic acid. WORD OF CAUTION: This trail is the entrance trail to a campground so be aware and YIELD to hikers. Keep your speed under control, observe all signs and be a friendly person.

After your ride, go back to the main park road and take a right down to the swimming area. The sandy beach with its big shade trees is a bit hypnotic...don't be surprised if you stay all day. For grub, try Sidesaddle Bakehouse in at 1111 W 290 in Dripping Springs. They have all the Texas favorites – King Ranch chicken, catfish with jalepeño hushpuppies, and awesome homemade bread. This county is dry, so you'll have to fend for yourself in the *cerveza* department.

How to get there - Take MoPac south to 290 West towards Johnson City. Go 12 miles past Dripping Springs (through Henley) and take a right on RR3232. Follow this 6 miles until it dead ends and go right then left into the park. Pay your $4/person at the ranger station and get your car pass.

67

Pedernales Falls State Park

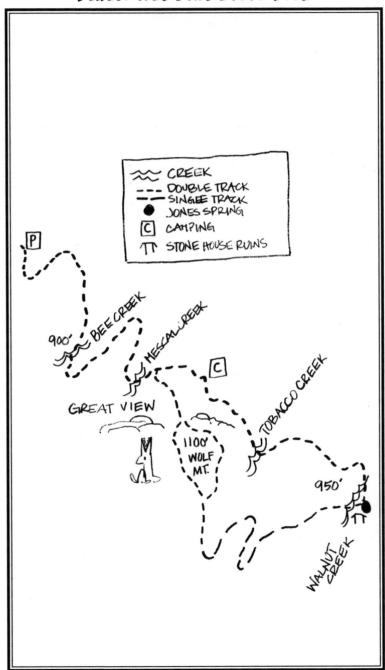

Kelly Creek Ranch
Intermediate/Difficult

Start:	The Bike Shop in Hunt, TX
Length:	25-30 miles of trails
Contact:	The owners (830) 367-5963; 896-6900; CALL FIRST

This 1200 acre ranch is in the heart of one of the prettiest areas in Texas. Surrounded by summer camps and weekend lodges, this part of the hill country is world famous for its rough beauty. The ranch boasts some great hills, its share of rocks and an eyeful (or even two eyes full) of views. It is fairly demanding, but basically a truly sweet knobby-headed experience.

The trails are a mixture of single track, rough jeep roads and semi-smooth jeep roads. There is some fantastic technical single track that winds around through the oaks and cedars, incorporating rocks and creek crossings. Once you reach the bottom of a gully be prepared to get in that granny to get back out. Conversely, once you get on top of some of the smoother jeep roads you can use all of the other end bombing back down!

Because of the hills and amount of trails it is possible to get a little confused so use the radio tower and power lines to help you get your bearings. For that very reason, they won't let you ride alone here.

After your legs can't go any more it its essential to go swimming and stuff your gut. The place to chow and grab a cold one is The Store in Hunt. It was on your right side when you drove in. It has some great food and a true hill country atmosphere.

Some of the best spots to swim in the Guadalupe river are on HWY 39. When heading back to Austin from Hunt there is a public area at the second river crossing with some small rapids if the conditions are right. A little further down, before you get to Ingram, you'll see the Ingram Dam on your right. If you've never been "dam sliding" you're not a true Texan so stop off and test your prowess and then soak in the river.

How to get there - This trip is about 105 miles and takes about 2 hours and 15 minutes. Take MoPac South to 290 West and go through Johnson City to Fredricksberg. Go into town and take a left onto 16 South to Kerrville. In Kerrville take a right onto 27 West to Ingram. In Ingram go straight at the Y onto 39 West and head to Hunt. Two miles past Ingram turn left at the Waltonia Lodges. Follow this road for a little over 3 miles to the Kelly Creek Ranch on the right. Check in at the wood-framed house and pay $5.

Kelly Creek Ranch

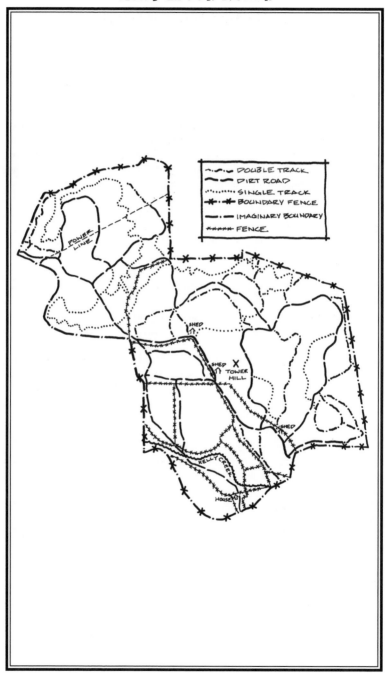

Somerville Trailway
Intermediate/Difficult

Start:	Outside of Giddings, TX
Length:	13 miles point to point, 26 total
Contact:	(979) 289-2392
Website:	www.tpwd.state.tx.us/park/lakesome/lakesome.htm

This is the perfect trail to hit for a phatt ride when you want a long distance work out. The scenic double track connects Nails Creek and Birch Creek State Parks as it goes around Flag Pond and the end of Lake Somerville. Alternating between mowed jeep track and maintained jeep-width trails the terrain is fairly smooth with no big rocks to interrupt your cadence.

There are some nice rolling hills mixed in with the flats and for about half the ride you are under a sweet tree canopy. The course is neither too hilly nor technical, which gives you plenty of time to soak up the scenery. (We promise you'll see some wildlife.)

The main challenge here is the length of the trail. Make sure you CALL before you go because this trail floods out sometimes. We know you've learned by now and we don't need to say it, but...as always, ride with caution because you are sharing the trail with hikers and equestrians.

If you need a swim at the half-way point, take a right out of the parking lot where the trail ends at Birch Creek State Park and look for the map that shows where to find lake access. Otherwise, you'll definitely want to hit the lake when you get back to Nails Creek State Park (you'll deserve it after 26 miles.)

When it comes time to refuel your stomach and soul, go about 1.5 miles out of the park to D's Entertainment Center on the right for some catfish and libations.

How to get there - (1.5 hours, 72 miles) Take MoPac north to the 2222/Northland exit and go right on Northland. Northland runs into 290 East, which you will take to Giddings. About 5 miles after Giddings take a left on 180, which will dead end at the Nails Creek State Park in about 12 miles. The cost is $2 per person and the office is open from 8-5 everyday with maps available in the office.

Somerville Trailway

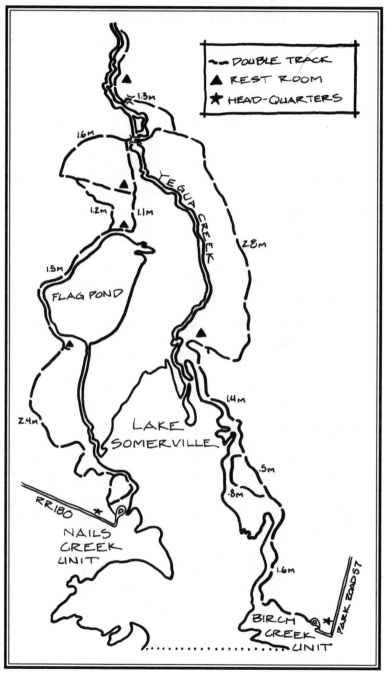

Bluff Creek Ranch
Intermediate/Difficult

Start:	Outside of Warda, TX; CALL FIRST
Length:	8 mile loop
Contact:	(979) 242-5894
Website:	www.bcrwarda.com

This relatively smooth eight mile loop is one of the most rideable around and gives all levels of bikers a good shred. The course is pretty flat and fast so intermediates feel like studs and advanced riders can go hard in the corners and ride out the 2-wheel drifts. The trail is almost all snake-turn single track through the pines and the terra is soft sandy loam with a few small rocks thrown in. There are many seasonal creek/runoff crossings with small bridges and logs placed across some for erosion purposes. The trail is excellently marked and maintained through out. There is no need for directions, but be careful on "Gas Pass" and "Oh Shit."

It costs $5.50 per person to ride all day and $7.50 to ride and camp. They have a real bathroom and a shower, which is there for everyone to use. The strong-backed budget-minded can take advantage of the "work for ride" .

For chow and libations, the place to hang out is the Warda Store - home of the famous Wardaburger. This joint consists of a store, gas station, post office and most importantly, restaurant and bar. The hamburgers are excellent and the beer is cold. The locals come here after work and the atmosphere is small town Texas - perfect after a hard ride. They are open normal hours except on Sunday when they are closed from 11:30-4:00.

How to get there - The trip is about 60 miles though and takes a little over an hour. From Austin High take 1st street east to I-35. Turn left (north) on the access road and take it to 7th street. Turn right on 7th veering left to Hwy 71 East after you cross the Colorado River. Go through the blackland prairie into the piney woods and continue through Bastrop about 11 miles to the Smithville exit. Exit and go left on FM153 East. You'll pass Rocky Hill with the old bike swinging in the wind, but you should save it for another day.

Continue on FM153 through Winchester until you dead end on Hwy 77. Go left on Hwy 77 about 4 miles to Warda. Take a right on Owl Creek (dirt) Road just after the store. Go .5 miles to the "Bluff Creek Ranch" entrance on the left and take the road back to the barn.

Bluff Creek Ranch

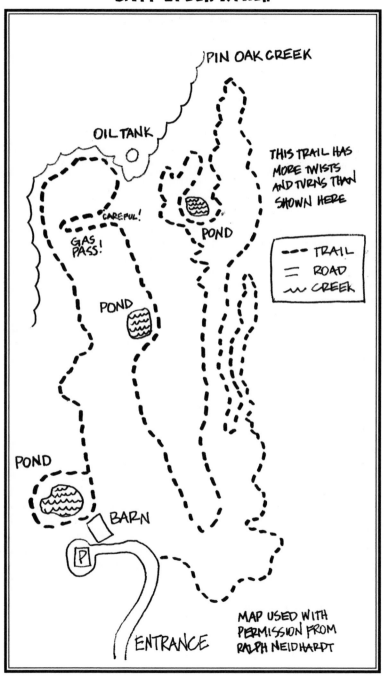

PIN OAK CREEK

OIL TANK

THIS TRAIL HAS
MORE TWISTS
AND TURNS THAN
SHOWN HERE

CAREFUL!

GAS
PASS!

POND

- - - TRAIL
= ROAD
~~ CREEK

POND

POND

BARN

P

ENTRANCE

MAP USED WITH
PERMISSION FROM
RALPH NEIDHARDT

Lake Bryan
Intermediate/Difficult

Start:	Near College Station
Length:	17 miles
Contact:	(979) 209-5200
Website:	http://bvmba.txcyber.com/trail_report.htm

There are two loops at the lake. The West loop is 8 miles and the harder of the two. The East loop is 9 miles and not as hard, but still challenging. Call ahead to make sure it's not wet and use some Slime tubes with sealant in them.

The E and W loops are fairly smooth, tight and twisty single track with a few short, straight double track spurts on the levy. The sections along the levy repeatedly drop steeply off the dam and then quickly return back up in granny gear fashion. Part of the terrain is loose, sandy soil that makes for great two wheel drifts, or diggers if that's your pleasure. Other sections are on darker soil that offers more gription and really lets you swing the bike. The roofing varies from tight forest to short open areas and there are some creek crossings.

After you have taken all the laps you can handle and then gone one more, the lake awaits to re-energize you for the drive into College Station to fill the belly. Out of the park take a left on 1687 to 2818. Go right on 2818 for about 6 miles and then left onto 60 towards campus. About 1.5 down on your left is Freebirds World Burritos. These burritos do the trick and even come in Super Monster size for you chow hounds. If you can walk after you are done, go next door to the Dixie Chicken for some foam and a dose of gig'em.

How to get there – This trip takes about two hours from Austin. Take 7th street east until it hits 183 and go south on 183. Take the HY71 exit on your left and head east to Bastrop. Outside of Bastrop turn left onto 21 and go through Caldwell towards Aggie land. 0.7 miles past the Little Brazos River go left on OSR (County Line Road.) Go 4 miles and take a right at the stop sign on FR1687 (Sandy Point Road.) The entrance to the park is 1.3 miles down on your left. Pay your fee and head to the left into the boat ramp parking lot. The trail head is away from the ramp at the start of the levy.

The price is $5 per car and the park is open from 6am-10pm. Camping is also available.

A special thanks goes to Rob Myer for the sweet map.

Lake Bryan

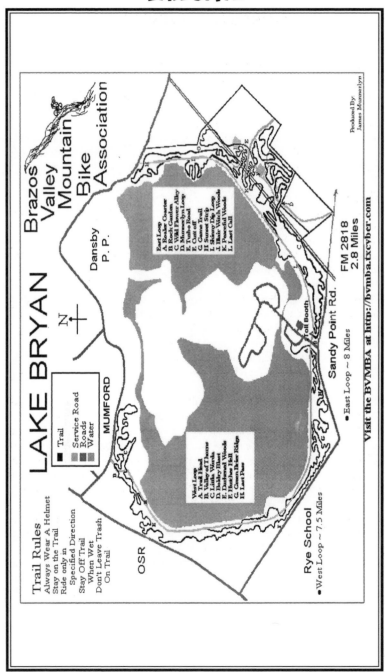

LAKE BRYAN

Brazos Valley Mountain Bike Association

Trail Rules
Always Wear A. Helmet
Stay on the Trail
Ride only in Specified Direction
Stay Off Trail When Wet
Don't Leave Trash On Trail

Dansby P. P.

MUMFORD

OSR

Legend
Trail
Service Road
Roads
Water

N

East Loop
A. Roeder Quarter
B. Rock Garden
C. Wild Flower Alley
D. Mumerlyn Loop
E. Turbo Road
F. Cutt off
G. Game Trail
H. Sunset Strip
I. Shiny Dip Loop
J. Bair Witch Woods
K. Bair Witch Woods
L. Last Call

West Loop
A. Trail Head
B. Valley of Thorns
C. Little Woods
D. Bobby Blast
E. Darkened Woods
F. Hatches Hell
G. Cross Brier Ridge
H. Last Pass

Sandy Point Rd.

FM 2818
2.8 Miles

Toll Booth

- East Loop ~ 8 Miles
- West Loop ~ 7.5 Miles

Rye School

Produced By:
James Mumnerlyn

Visit the BVMBA at http://bvmba.txcyber.com

Cameron State Park
Intermediate/Difficult

Start:	In Waco
Length:	About 30 miles last count
Contact:	Waco Parks and Recreation (817) 750-8080
Website:	www.waco-texas.com/city-depts/parks/parksdiv.htm

How can you not have fun on semi smooth, tree-covered single track combined with short, steep hills and a sprinkle of jumps? This maze of trails, the map showing the main ones, offers some great Central Texas riding. Go ride it!

The park is about 500 acres and there are lots of roads, which makes getting lost a little harder and exploring trails easier. These sweet trails are almost 100% single track with very few rocks. The terrain varies from plush river bottom to short, steep climbs that twist through cottonwoods and creek beds. The trails between Lawson's and Circle Point are nice and rolly with some good Mr. Twister tracks.

There are some technical, rocky, run-off sections on the really steep stuff, so be prepared. Some of the best trails shoot you through the banked-turned gullies that require many runs to truly appreciate. All in all this park is a blast to ride and will keep you busy trying to learn all of the trails. William Cameron donated this 416 acre park for the "perpetual enjoyment of the people" so do what the man requested!

Buzzard Billy's Armadillo Bar-N-Grill is the spot to munch and sip suds after riding. To get there, get back on University Parks Drive as if you were heading home. After you cross Franklin Street, pull a U-turn before the railroad tracks and you'll so it on your right. It is a 1930s warehouse with some really cool old bikes (some with front shocks) hanging from the ceiling. The food is Cajun with a wide range of options, including Creole fettuccine. There are over 30 kinds of beers and many of them are on tap.

How to get there – The 95 mile trip takes about 1.5 hours. Take MoPac north all the way to I-35. (MoPac turns into 1325 and then I-35.) Get on I-35 North all the way to Waco. Once in Waco, take the University Parks exit and go left on University Parks Drive, which leads to the entrance of the park. Enter the park and take Cameron Park Drive along the river and park at the Rock Shelter on your right (before the road goes uphill into the woods.)

Cameron State Park

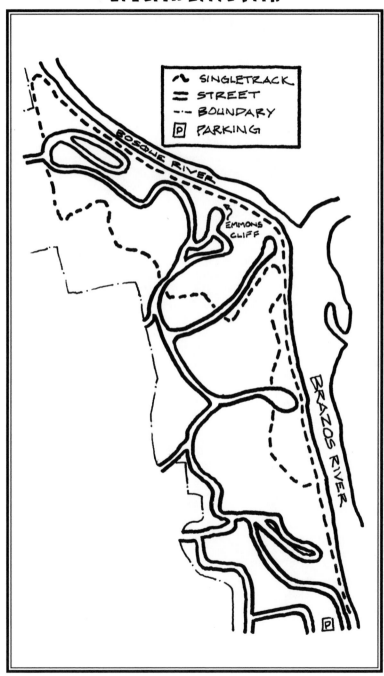

X-Bar Ranch
Intermediate/Difficult

Start:	Live Oak Lodge
Length:	3, 9 & 12 mile loops
Contact:	(888) 853-2688 or (915) 853-2688. YOU MUST CALL AHEAD (trail use is restricted during hunting seasons)
Website:	www.XbarRanch.com

This 1,850 acre West Texas ranch has a network of 3 challenging loops that extend off of each other. The terrain is a mix of rocky limestone, cedar hillsides, oak monts and mesquite flats. The maximum elevation drop on the ranch is about 150' so none of the climbs are very long. There are only a few rocky technical sections, but you have to stay focused the whole ride as you consistently weave through the rocks on the hillsides and creekbed sections.

Most of the trials are single track with a little double track thrown in. The middle ring single track on the hillsides is tight, twisty, and pretty rocky. There are some flat, semi-smooth ridgeline sections between the accents and descents to give you a breather. At the lower elevation of the ranch you enter the mesquite flats that are smooth and a little sandy. In here the single track opens up and you can pick up some speed. The short double track offers a good change of pace and you can work the big ring a little but there are no extended high speed sections. From here you ride back into the fun single track, across the flats, and then climb to the trailhead.

At the trailhead by the cabins there is a conveniently located pool over-looking the valley where you can cool off after hammering out some miles. If you stay in the cabins, you can cook inside the lodge or BBQ outside. If you go into Sonora, the Stagecoach Grill is the place to gorge. To get there, drive back to Sonora and go into town on 277 south. At the T, turn left towards Del Rio and the Grill is 0.5 miles down on your left. You might want to go early because the *cabrito* goes fast, but the beer will not run out.

How to get there – This 3.5 hour drive, coupled with its beautifully remote location and fun trails, merits spending the night in our opinion. It's $5 for day riders. For information on lodging & camping, please visit their website. Take 290 all the way to I 10 and go West on I 10 to Sonora. Go through Sonora and take Exit 388 onto FM 1312. Go West on 1312 1.8 miles and take a right on FM 2129 going East. The Live Oak Lodge is about 7 miles up the hill on the right.

X-Bar Ranch

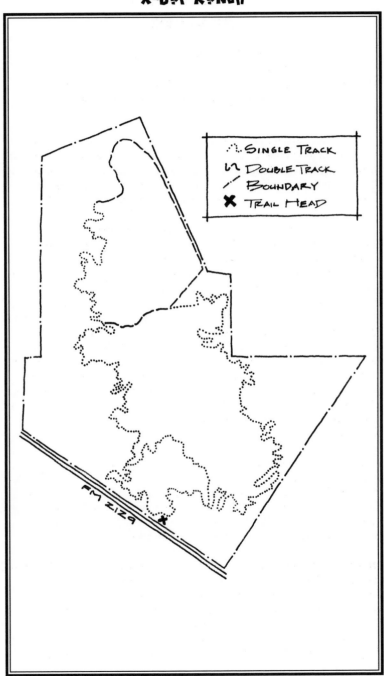

Flat Rock Ranch
All Levels

Start: Outside of Comfort, TX
Length: 18 miles
Contact: Jimmy Dreiss (830) 995-2858 or (210) 213-3006.
                   Closed during hunting season so call ahead!
Website: http://www.flatrockranch.net

This 1,300 acre ranch has excellent riding and offers a nice change of pace compared to most other Central Texas rides. The main difference is that there are some long climbs, which translates into great descents. Some of the single track is more open and you can carry a lot of big ring speed as you fly down the hills. They even have a dedicated downhill course!

There are 2 main 9 mile loops that meet near the parking area. There are also some shorter options for beginning riders. Most the trails are single track with some jeep roads mixed in. Some of the single track was created by cows and some man made. The combo flows very well and allows you to carry speed. If you only have the time, or stamina, to ride one loop we suggest riding the lower pasture. The loop starts of with some good climbing and nice switchbacks. When you make it to the top (you will know it), take the time to look back at the great view. From here hang on! The trail traverses and offers some great flowing downhills. When you get back to the creek you can get food or water at your car if you need to, or you can hammer into the upper pasture loop. After you work you way through the bottomland and creek crossings, you head back up and there are some steep climbing sections with more rocks than the other loop. Once again, the gain is much more than the pain as you get to haul butt down! If you like to go fast, this is the place.

If the creek at the ranch is flowing, there are a few spots to cool off. For a swim in the Guadalupe, take I-10 South and after a few miles you will get to the river. To get some good grub & suds, Double D is the place. Go back the way you came but when 473 hits 87 go left, or South, on 87. At the stop sign go left on 27 and Double D will be on your left. They have a wide selection of food and beer and the burgers are good.

How to get there: This trip takes about 2 hours and is $5. Take 290 West and just outside of Fredericksburg take a left on Friendship Lane. Friendship lane is located at the light by Wal-Mart. At the stop sign, go left on 87 South (S. Washington). Go 21 miles on 87 toward Comfort. At the flashing light go left on 473 for one mile. Turn left on Flat Rock Creek Road. After 4 miles the pavement ends at the gate to the ranch. Go through the gate, CLOSE THE GATE and park near the first house on the left.

Flat Rock Ranch
All Levels

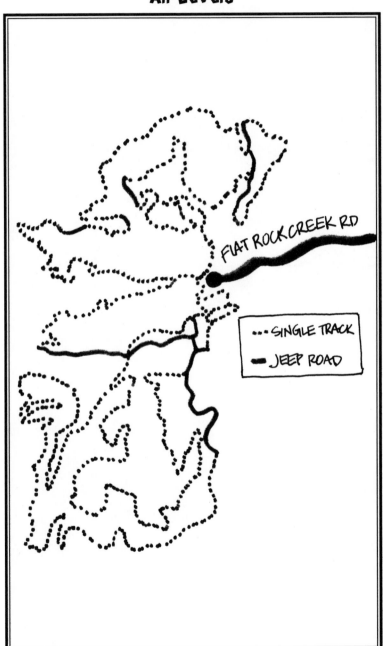

Walnut Creek

Austin Locator Map

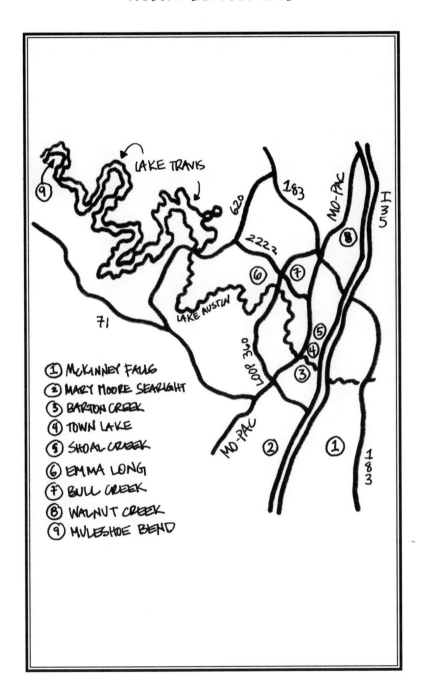

LAKE TRAVIS

① McKINNEY FALLS
② MARY MOORE SEARIGHT
③ BARTON CREEK
④ TOWN LAKE
⑤ SHOAL CREEK
⑥ EMMA LONG
⑦ BULL CREEK
⑧ WALNUT CREEK
⑨ MULESHOE BEND

Emma Long

Day Trip Locator Map

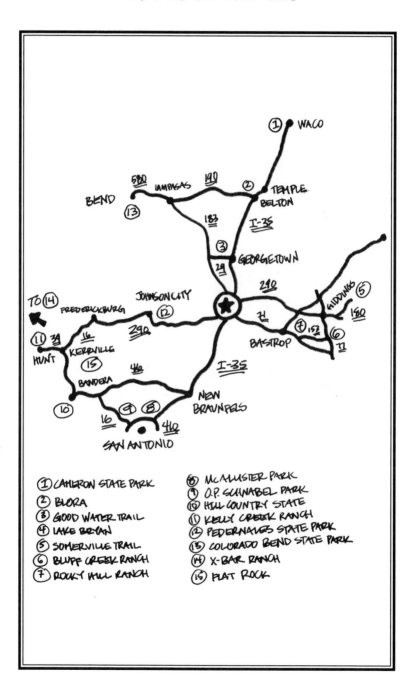

① CAMERON STATE PARK
② BLORA
③ GOOD WATER TRAIL
④ LAKE BRYAN
⑤ SOMERVILLE TRAIL
⑥ BLUFF CREEK RANCH
⑦ ROCKY HILL RANCH

⑧ MCALLISTER PARK
⑨ O.P. SCHNABEL PARK
⑩ HILL COUNTRY STATE
⑪ KELLY CREEK RANCH
⑫ PEDERNALES STATE PARK
⑬ COLORADO BEND STATE PARK
⑭ X-BAR RANCH
⑮ FLAT ROCK

ALPHABETICAL LIST OF RIDES

RIDES BY DIFFUCULTY LEVEL

Ride	Level	Page Number
BLORA/Trailblazer MBP	All levels	58
Colorado Bend State Park	All levels	52
Rocky Hill Ranch	All levels	54
Good Water Trail	All levels	60
Hill Country St. Natural Area	All levels	56
Flat Rock Ranch	All levels	80
Mary Moore Searight Park	Easy	36
Shoal Creek Greenbelt	Easy	34
Town Lake Hike-and-Bike	Easy	32
McAllister Park	Easy/Inter	62
McKinney Falls State Park	Easy/Inter	40
O.P. Schnabel Park	Easy/Inter	64
Bull Creek Greenbelt	Easy/Inter	38
Walnut Creek Greenbelt	Easy/Inter	46
Barton Creek Greenbelt	Intermediate	42
Pedernales State Park	Intermediate	66
Bluff Creek Ranch	Inter/Difficult	72
Cameron State Park	Inter/Difficult	76
Kelly Creek Ranch	Inter/Difficult	68

Ride	Level	Page Number
Lake Bryan	Inter/Difficult	74
Muleshoe Bend	Inter/Difficult	44
Somerville Trailway	Inter/Difficult	70
X-Bar Ranch	Inter/Difficult	78
Emma Long Motocross Park	Difficult	48

ORDER FORM

This book is a great gift!

Fill out the order form below and send it (with the jack, Jack) to:

Ragged Edge Riders
P.O. Box 161862
Austin, TX 78716

◆◆

Please send me _____book(s) at $9.95 each. $ _____

Here is $3.00 for shipping and handling. $_____
(Good for up to five books.)

Total: $_____

Here is my check or money order, payable to **Ragged Edge Riders**. No cash, credit cards, or COD orders accepted.

Send the book(s) to me at:

Name: _____

Address: _____

City: _____

State: _____

Zip: _____

Phone: _____ Email:_____

ORDER FORM

This book is a great gift!

Fill out the order form below and send it (with the jack, Jack) to:

Ragged Edge Riders
P.O. Box 161862
Austin, TX 78716

◆◆◆

Please send me _____book(s) at $9.95 each. $ _____

Here is $3.00 for shipping and handling. $_____
(Good for up to five books.)

                 Total: $_____

Here is my check or money order, payable to **Ragged Edge Riders**. No cash, credit cards, or COD orders accepted.

Send the book(s) to me at:

Name: _____

Address: _____

City: _____

State: _____

Zip: _____

Phone: _____ Email:_____

RIDE SUGGESTION FORM

Have you ridden a new trail?

If you have found any new trails, we'd dig hearing about them. If you have any new scoop on trails that are in here we would like to hear about that too.

Please fill out the form below and send it to us at:

Ragged Edge Riders

P.O. Box 161862
Austin, TX 78716

◆◆

Here's the scoop on the trail:

_____

_____

_____

_____

_____

If you have questions you can contact me at:

Name: _____

Address: _____

_____

Phone: _____

Email: _____

RIDE SUGGESTION FORM

Have you ridden a new trail?

If you have found any new trails, we'd dig hearing about them. If you have any new scoop on trails that are in here we would like to hear about that too.

Please fill out the form below and send it to us at:

Ragged Edge Riders
P.O. Box 161862
Austin, TX 78716

◆◆◆

Here's the scoop on the trail:

_____

_____

_____

_____

_____

If you have questions you can contact me at:

Name: _____

Address: _____

_____

Phone: _____

Email: _____

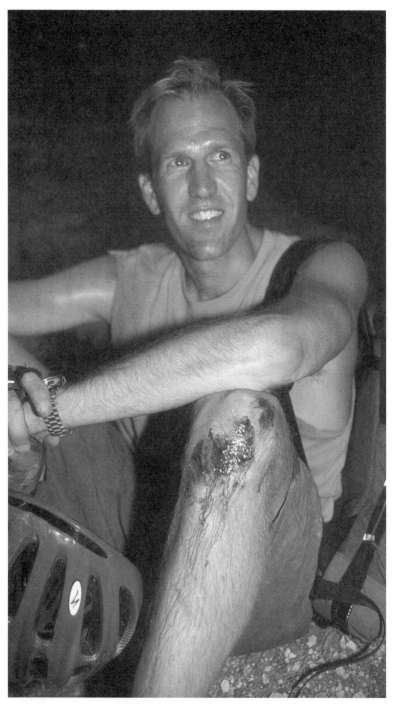

Blood, Sweat & Gears

RIDE LOG

As epic as that ride was that you did yesterday, chances are you won't remember it if you don't write it down.

This is not a training log. You can write that hard-core, be like Lance stuff down somewhere else. This is a place to record great experiences so that you can glance at them and recall the time shared riding with buddies.

We started doing this a while ago and wish we had been jotting this stuff down from the time that we started biking. It's really cool to look back over your best and/or most fun rides.

Fill these out over big burritos after the ride or in the car while you're road tripping home. You'll be glad you did.

RIDE LOG

Ride Name: _____

Date: _____ Temperature: _____

Riding Buddies: _____

Trail Conditions: _____

My Condition: _____

Biff of the Day:_____
_____
_____
_____
_____

Schweet Move of the Day: _____
_____
_____
_____
_____

Comentarios: _____
_____
_____
_____
_____
_____
_____

Post Ride Schnanigans: _____
_____
_____
_____

RIDE LOG

Ride Name: _____

Date: _____ Temperature: _____

Riding Buddies: _____

Trail Conditions: _____

My Condition: _____

Biff of the Day: _____
_____
_____
_____
_____

Schweet Move of the Day: _____
_____
_____
_____
_____

Comentarios: _____
_____
_____
_____
_____
_____
_____

Post Ride Schnanigans: _____
_____
_____
_____

98

RIDE LOG

Ride Name: _____

Date: _____ Temperature: _____

Riding Buddies: _____

Trail Conditions: _____

My Condition: _____

Biff of the Day:_____
_____
_____
_____
_____

Schweet Move of the Day: _____
_____
_____
_____
_____

Comentarios: _____
_____
_____
_____
_____
_____
_____

Post Ride Schnanigans: _____
_____
_____
_____
_____

RIDE LOG

Ride Name: _____

Date: _____ Temperature: _____

Riding Buddies: _____

Trail Conditions: _____

My Condition: _____

Biff of the Day:_____
_____
_____
_____
_____

Schweet Move of the Day: _____
_____
_____
_____
_____

Comentarios: _____
_____
_____
_____
_____
_____
_____

Post Ride Schnanigans: _____
_____
_____
_____
_____

The MAD House

www.the-mad-house.com

Advertising. Design. Results.

The McIntosh Advertising and Design House, Inc.
o. 512/502-9595 f. 512/502-9722 e. advertise@the-mad-house.com

Southwest Regional
CANCER CENTER

CONGRATULATES LANCE ARMSTRONG!

IMBA Rules of the Trail

1. Ride on open trails only.
2. Leave no trace.
3. Control your bicycle.
4. Always yield the trail.
5. Never spook animals.
6. Plan ahead.

I·M·B·A

INTERNATIONAL MOUNTAIN BIKING ASSOCIATION

A non-profit, public-supported organization. The mission of IMBA is to promote mountain bicycling opportunities that are environmentally sound and socially responsible.

Join • Learn • Ride: 303-545-9011 • www.imba.com